PÉREZ GALD

Tristana

Lisa Pauline Condé

Senior Lecturer in Spanish
University of Wales, Swansea

London
Grant & Cutler Ltd
2000

© Grant & Cutler Ltd 2000

ISBN 0 7293 0418 3

10019854 33

DEPÓSITO LEGAL: V. 1.164 - 2000

605157

Printed in Spain by
Artes Gráficas Soler, S.L., Valencia
for
GRANT & CUTLER LTD
55–57 GREAT MARLBOROUGH STREET, LONDON W1V 2AY

Contents

For my mother

Preface

All references to the text of *Tristana* are taken from Gordon Minter's annotated edition (Bristol: Bristol Classical Press, 1996), with page numbers following in parentheses. References to other works by Galdós, unless indicated otherwise, are taken from the Obras Completas edited by Federico Carlos Sainz de Robles (Madrid: Aguilar, 1971), using the following abbreviations: *OC* (*Obras Completas*), *NI*, *NII*, *NIII* (*Novelas* I, *Novelas* II, *Novelas* III) or CTC (Cuentos, Teatro y Censo), followed by the page number.

The figures in parentheses in italic type refer to the numbered items in the Bibliographical Note; where appropriate these are followed by page numbers.

Occasional reference is made to copy manuscript and galley proofs of *Tristana* held in the Casa-Museo Pérez Galdós in Las Palmas in Caja 19, Núm. 1, to the original manuscript held in the Biblioteca Nacional in Madrid, MS 21791, and also to letters from Concha-Ruth Morell in Las Palmas, Caja 10, Carp. 37–38, Legajo 105.

I should like to thank all the staff of the Casa-Museo in Las Palmas for their kind assistance when consulting material, Professor Alan Deyermond for his painstaking editing, and Mr Stephen Cooper for his patience and guidance.

I should especially like to remember Professor John Varey in gratitude for the help and kindness he afforded me over the years and for encouraging me in the preparation of this Critical Guide on *Tristana*.

1. Introduction

Galdós's polemical novel of 1892, *Tristana*, has recently been receiving increased critical attention. A new translation of the text into English with an additional section on Buñuel's film version by Colin Partridge appeared in 1995 (*25*); Gordon Minter produced a most welcome critical edition of the original text in 1996 (*22*); and in 1997 Aitor Bikandi-Mejías published a comparative study on the novel and the film (*5*). Numerous articles on *Tristana* have appeared over the last few years and debates on this text at conferences at home and abroad have become increasingly heated. The novel has been gaining popularity in university courses on Galdós, and the time for a Critical Guide seems propitious. Because Tristana provokes so much debate, an objective analysis is neither easy nor, perhaps, desirable. My own views will, therefore, undoubtedly surface, although the other side of the argument will also be given.

Galdós clearly had strong views on a number of issues although, as a 'realist' writer, the aim was to present at least 'an appearance of objectivity' if not quite achieving 'the objective representation of contemporary reality' demanded by René Wellek.[1] In *Tristana*, however, the author's views are virtually impossible to determine as this text is particularly and, it would seem, deliberately ambiguous.

Galdós himself stressed that 'la vida del hombre y el trabajo del artista van tan íntimamente ligados, y se compenetran de tal modo, que no hay manera de que por separado se produzcan, sin afectarse mutuamente'.[2] Nevertheless, many modern critics insist that a text be read and interpreted in isolation, i.e. without regard for the author or his/her social circumstances. While a text must clearly

---

[1] Wellek, 'The Concept of Realism in Literary Scholarship', *Concepts of Criticism* (New Haven: Yale UP, 1963), p. 240.
[2] B. Pérez Galdós, *Arte y Crítica* (Madrid: Renacimiento, 1923), p. 109.

stand on its own, it is my view that in some cases, including that of *Tristana*, knowledge of both the writer and the context can add to our appreciation of the work and I shall, therefore, devote a little time and space to their consideration.

Benito Pérez Galdós (1843–1920) is widely acclaimed as Spain's greatest writer since Cervantes and as a major figure in European realism.[3] Most renowned for his *novelas contemporáneas*, Galdós was the author of a number of political and literary articles and reviews, forty-six *Episodios Nacionales*, thirty-one novels and twenty-two published plays. His achievements as 'the creator of the modern novel in Spain', 'a social historian', and variations on the theme of 'a literary social psychologist' have been the subject of considerable discussion in an ever-expanding bibliography.[4]

The recent growth of feminist studies has led to further examination of the depiction of women in Galdós's work which, to some extent, has coincided with a resurgence of interest in the plays written and performed between 1892 (the year of *Tristana)* and 1918. This is of particular relevance as it is through his contemporary drama that Galdós realizes his idea of a 'mujer nueva' who, unlike the frustrated victims of his novels, takes control. *Tristana* can be seen as a novel of dilemma insofar as 'the woman question'[5] is

---

[3] See J. P. Stern, *On Realism* (London: Routledge & Kegan Paul, 1973), who describes Galdos's novel, *Fortunata y Jacinta*, as 'unquestionably a European masterpiece' p.190.

[4] See respectively L. B. Walton, *Pérez Galdós and the Spanish Novel of the Nineteenth Century* (New York: Gordian Press, 1970 [first published London, 1927]), p.viii; Gerald Brenan, *The Literature of the Spanish People* (Cambridge: Cambridge University Press, 1976 [first published Cambridge, 1951, p. 404]); and Sherman Eoff, *The Novels of Pérez Galdós: The Concept of Life as Dynamic Process* (St Louis: Washington University Press, 1954), p. 3.

[5] Cf. Chapter 2 of Catherine Jagoe's study (*12*), entitled 'Galdós and the Woman Question'. Emilia Pardo Bazán wrote in 1892, the year of *Tristana*: 'Es la llamada *cuestión de la mujer* acaso la más seria entre las que hoy se agitan' (*24*, p. 156). The issue was much debated in England and the United States, leading to the publication of such articles as that by Grant Allen, 'Plain Words on the Woman Question', *Fortnightly Review*, 46 (1889),

concerned, particularly as the ending is so ambiguous, and has led some critics to declare both the novel and its author 'anti-feminist'.[6]

The woman question is a highly pertinent one in Galdós studies, as is apparent from the titles of so many of his novels and plays. From relatively recently acquired information about the writer's personal experiences with women, it is clear that such relationships were crucial to the creation of much of his work and to the development of his ideas, and can add a further dimension to our appreciation of that creation, notwithstanding the independence of the text itself. Much of the heroine's dilemma in *Tristana* corresponds to that experienced by Galdós's mistress Concha-Ruth Morell and, indeed, much of the text consists of her letters to him 'literalmente copiadas', as the young actress herself complained.

Concha-Ruth was subsequently to play the role of Clotilde, who can be seen as the precursor to 'la mujer nueva' in Galdós's first staged play, *Realidad,* which opened at the Teatro de la Comedia in Madrid on 15 March 1892. Much was going on in this year, as the next chapter will show.

In literary terms, Galdós had been anxious to break away from the Romanticism of the early part of the nineteenth century and promote a more faithful 'imagen de la vida' through the novel, which he believed 'debe ser enseñanza, ejemplo' rather than empty entertainment.[7] His early, largely anti-clerical novels, while not without art, have been described as 'thesis novels', while those of his 'segunda manera' (the 'novelas contemporáneas') are those for which he has been most acclaimed. *Tristana* appears towards the end

---

455–56, and 'The New Aspect of the Woman Question', *North American Review,* 158 (1894), 271–73. See Sally Ledger, 'The New Woman and the Crisis of Victorianism' in *Cultural Politics at the 'Fin de siècle'* (Cambridge: Cambridge University Press, 1998), pp. 22–44.

[6] Notably Leon Livingstone (*18*). Catherine Jagoe also considers that Galdós 'appropriates aspects of feminist discourse, such as the term "new woman", in the service of a conservative class agenda' (*16*, p. 182).

[7] The first quotation is from Pérez Galdós, *Discursos leídos ante la Real Academia Española* (Madrid, 1897), pp. 11–12, and the second is Pérez Galdós quoted by Luis Antón del Olmet & Arturo García Carraffa, *Los grandes españoles,* I : *Galdós* (Madrid, 1912), p. 93.

of this second period, during a time of change on many levels. By this point, Galdós had already fully realized the potential of the realist novel and was experimenting with alternative forms of artistic expression, including the dialogue novel, the epistolary novel, and the play. He was also influenced by contemporary movements towards more directly spiritual concerns which he was to pursue in later novels, although the majority of his contemporary plays continued to focus on practical and social, as well as moral and psychological, issues.

Tristana is a relatively short novel which did not receive much attention at the time of its publication. Possibly one of the reasons for this was that its irony was not fully appreciated, being so far from the overt irony of Galdós's earlier novel, *Doña Perfecta,* and another reason was probably the fact that its publication coincided so closely with his dramatic début with *Realidad,* on which all attention was focused. *Tristana* was certainly never considered a masterpiece of the stature of *Fortunata y Jacinta* (1888–89), although the novelist Emilia Pardo Bazán (Galdós's close friend and former mistress) believed that it had the potential of being 'quizá la mejor novela de Galdós' (*24*, p. 137) had the ending been different. Buñuel, of course, radically changed the ending of the work for his film version, which will be considered in Chapter 7.

It was Buñuel's film version of *Tristana* in 1970 which first revived critical interest in the novel, to be further fuelled by a period of active feminism. While attention first focused on the feminist theme of Galdós's work (and to some extent this focus has persisted, in the absence of any consensus on the issue), the novel's irony, ambiguity, and indeterminacy have increasingly been seen in positive rather than negative terms, generating further critical attention. Studies have also mushroomed on the wealth of literary allusions and what Germán Gullón describes as 'literaturización' in this text (*14*), as well as on the significance of the role of art and the concept of desire. Indeed, *Tristana* is now recognized as an eminently modern literary production of great narratological complexity further incorporating, as Joan Grimbert has recently stressed, 'subversion as a major thematic and structural component' (*13,* p. 109).

While some critics concluded that the apparently hasty, inconclusive and therefore unsatisfactory ending of the novel was partly due to Galdós's preoccupation with his forthcoming dramatic début with *Realidad*, the manuscripts and galley-proofs available in the Casa-Museo Pérez Galdós in Las Palmas and the Biblioteca Nacional in Madrid indicate that he devoted a considerable amount of care and attention to the writing, re-writing, and emending of this novel, notwithstanding the fact that parts of the original manuscript contained scribbled notes relating to *Realidad*.[8] Galdós did, of course, invariably rework a lot of his material and parts of *Tristana* were emended quite radically, notably in the original manuscript, where Galdós considered: '¿Se corta la pierna de don Lope?', perhaps with the intention of persuading Tristana into the caring 'ángel del hogar' role by this means (as suggested by James Whiston, *38*), and subsequently proceeded to present 'el anciano galán' (a phrase coined at the last minute in the galley-proofs) in a somewhat more sympathetic light than he had initially intended. However, the galley-proofs show an exceptional amount of reworking in Galdós's hand on every sheet, indicating that this novel was not hastily brushed aside in favour of the production of *Realidad*.

Among the issues Galdós focuses on in *Tristana* is the question of identity, particularly with regard to the heroine and her quest for autonomy, and issues of gender, perception, and control will be explored accordingly. Narrative stance will be found to shift, adding to the task of the reader for, as the currently popular novelist, playwright, and film-maker Clive Barker confirms, a good novel is 'at least as much yours (the reader's) as the author's'.[9] Barker stresses the fact that there is less room for ambiguity in a film, and this is apparent in the case of *Tristana.* We can be more sure of the

---

[8] The original manuscript of *Tristana* is housed in the Biblioteca Nacional, and a photocopy in the Casa-Museo Pérez Galdós, Caja 19, Núm. 1, as are the galley-proofs.

[9] Clive Barker interviewed on Radio 5 Live, 5 November 1998.

outcome in Buñuel's version of the work, regardless of our response to it. We can only guess and continue guessing in the case of the novel, which is far from straightforward and is related by a deliberately elusive narrator, who at times seems to be teasing us. The very ending of the novel, with the closing words, 'Tal vez ...' (111), appears set to keep us guessing, however closely we delve into the text.

On the other hand, delving into the text can prove very rewarding, as it is rich in terms of language, irony, literary allusions, and social, psychological, and philosophical dilemmas. Possible interpretations continue to multiply and it is the aim of this brief Guide to give a taste of some of these in the context of a general introduction to the work, and then to take a closer look at the feminist implications of *Tristana*. In particular, I should like to reconsider Marina Mayoral's assertion that 'Tristana se adelanta a su tiempo por sus ideas y no es comprendida' (*20*, p. 28), in the hope not only of underlining the modernity of this novel but also of taking a further step towards an understanding of its so misunderstood heroine.

2. 1892: A Time for Change

When *Tristana* was written, change was imminent as a new century approached, and reflection, anticipation, and apprehension were all in the air. In literary, philosophical, and political terms, Spain was on the move, as was Galdós on both the personal and the professional front. Some of this sense of 'ebullición' is apparent in *Tristana*. Restlessness and resistance to the status quo are discernible, in varying manner and degree, in all three main characters of this novel: don Lope, Tristana, and Horacio, who can be seen respectively to illustrate the reflection, anticipation, and apprehension mentioned above. The author himself no longer conforms exactly to what we have come to expect in terms of a realist novel, and the narrator is so elusive that we cannot pin him down at all.

The social realist novel, which had flourished in Spain and the rest of Europe during the second half of the nineteenth century, was now being affected by a movement towards more individual psychological and spiritual preoccupations in the manner of Tolstoy. To some extent this movement can be discerned in *Tristana*, although it is more apparent in some of Galdós's later novels such as *Nazarín*. Galdós himself was clearly in experimental mode, having published the epistolary novel *La incógnita* in 1889 and the dialogue novel *Realidad* in 1891, which he was subsequently to adapt for the stage in 1892, the year of *Tristana*. *Tristana* itself is a difficult novel to define, having elements of the social realist, the psychological, the epistolary, and what might loosely be termed experimental. It does have a fairly easily defined feminist theme, although not such an easily defined thesis or argument, but then it was clearly not written as another thesis novel.

Tristana is a novel which deals with possibilities of change and choice, particularly in regard to its eponymous heroine. Her sense of restlessness and frustration not only echoes that of Galdós's young lover, the actress Concha-Ruth Morell, but also, as Emilia Pardo Bazán was quick to point out, that of 'millones de almas oprimidas por el mismo horrible peso, a sabiendas o sin advertirlo' (*24*, p. 140). For despite the liberal ideas of the Revolution of 1868 and the Krausist philosophy which so influenced late-nineteenth-century intellectual thought in Spain, women were still constrained and marginalized, denied the education and opportunities afforded to their male counterparts. More is made of the need for change on this front in Galdós's novel than in Buñuel's film, although the latter does stress the limited nature of the choices available to Tristana as she ponders over which *garbanzo* to eat first or which column, out of two which are identical, she should select as being the better.

Galdós's stance, as evidenced by his writing, correspondence and political intervention, was essentially liberal with increasingly socialist overtones, and Carla Her has likened his views on women's roles in society to the early 'liberal feminism' of John Stuart Mill.[10] Emila Pardo Bazán was preparing an introduction to the Spanish translation of Mill's study *The Subjection of Women* at the time Galdós was writing *Tristana* and it is highly likely that they would have discussed her views. Ibsen's *A Doll's House* had also just been translated into Spanish, so the question was clearly a topical one at the time Galdós explored the concept of a more radical form of feminism in *Tristana*.[11]

Geraldine Scanlon explains that the term 'feminism' was coined in France around 1882 and spread rapidly to other countries, notably England, Germany and the United States (*27*, p. 4). In his study of *Feminismo*, however, published in Madrid in 1899, Adolfo González Posada maintained that in Spain 'no existía una polémica seria sobre cuestiones feministas' and that 'no se habían formado grupos feministas bien organizados con un programa de reformas

---

[10] Carla Her, 'Pérez Galdós, Pardo Bazán y Stuart Mill: una aproximación literaria y filosófica de la problemática femenina en el siglo XIX', *Actas del Tercer Congreso Internacional de Estudios Galdosianos* (Las Palmas: Cabildo Insular de Gran Canaria, 1989), 189–208.

[11] The translation of *A Doll's House* was published in *La España Moderna* (1889–1914), 44 (Aug. 1892), 131–70 and 45 (Sept. 1892), 18–65.

prácticas'. This was not to happen in Spain until the late 1920s. Furthermore, according to González Posada, 'los escritores y políticos habían demostrado poco interés por el tema y las manifestaciones del feminismo, o al menos los acontecimientos reseñables que expresaban un interés por la posición de las mujeres eran escasos: la labor de los krausistas en educación; los Congresos Pedagógicos de 1882 y 1892; la reforma de la Escuela Normal de Maestras; los comienzos de una literatura que trataba del feminismo (gran parte de la cual era anti-feminista) y, por último, las secciones especiales dedicadas al feminismo en algunas publicaciones periódicas, como la *Revista Política* y la *Revista Popular*'.[12]

Rhian Davies's recent dissertation on *La España Moderna* confirms that a considerable number of articles related to feminism were published in that journal including, of course, the famous study by Pardo Bazán on 'La mujer española', first published in English in the *Fortnightly Review* in June 1889. In a letter to Galdós, Pardo Bazán wrote: 'Yo estoy contenta de él pero es un poquito fuerte; armaría un alboroto en España tal vez si se publicase en español.'[13] Davies comments that she was probably surprised when Lázaro Galdiano (General Editor and founder of the journal, as well as her former lover) asked her to publish the article in *La España Moderna*.[14] The journal also published articles by Concepción Arenal and González Posada and subsequently, Davies observes, 'there were hardly any aspects relating to the position of women which *La España Moderna* did not explore'. She points out, however, that not all the ideas expressed in the journal were progressive, many being counterbalanced by the traditional, conservative ideas of the period, encapsulated in the words of Gómez de Baquero: 'Para el que tenga algún sedimento conservador en el espíritu, el feminismo es un tema triste, porque se ve en él la decadencia del hogar, y no sólo la desintegración de ese noble ideal

---

[12] Adolfo González Posada, *Feminismo* (Madrid: F. Fé, 1899), pp. 191–93.
[13] *Cartas a Benito Pérez Galdós de Emilia Pardo Bazán (1889–90)*, ed. Carmen Bravo-Villasante (Madrid: Ediciones Turner, 1975), p. 59.
[14] Rhian Davies, '*La España Moderna*: The Cultural Review and Spain (1889–1914)', unpublished dissertation, University of Oxford, 1996.

de la relación entre los sexos que fué el matrimonio cristiano, sino la debilitación de las instituciones familiares'.[15]

Davies stresses that not only were potential feminists strongly contested by the Church, which also argued that feminism threatened tradition and could destroy the family institution as well as the social and national life of Spain, but that most Spanish women had conservative views and, as they worked in isolation in the home or fields, they were not in a position to become collectively conscious of their oppression.

Nevertheless, it is clear that Galdós was concerned about the role of women in society throughout his writing career, and particularly concerned about the extremely limited education afforded to them. Following his arrival in Madrid at the age of nineteen to study at the University, he had soon found himself involved in the animated discussions taking place there and in the Ateneo on the ideas of the German philosopher, Krause, and his theories on education. Galdós's professor at the University, Julián Sanz del Río, had spent two years studying Krause's theories in Germany, and on his return to Spain spent the following ten years developing these ideas in an attempt to produce a practical system of education aimed at the fullest possible development of each individual's potential. Sanz took up his chair at the University in 1854, some eight years before Galdós' arrival, and soon inspired enthusiasm amongst his students. One of these, Francisco Giner de los Ríos, founded the Institución Libre de Enseñanza, based on this Krausist system, in 1876. One of the first autonomous institutions of learning in Spain, the Institución proved a considerable influence on several generations of great Spaniards.

Notwithstanding the recognized shortcomings of the Krausists' reliance on the power of reason to overcome all obstacles, their contribution to the field of education was far-reaching. Pierre Jobit describes their attitude towards the desirability of properly educating women:

---

[15] E. Gómez de Baquero, 'Crónica literaria', *La España Moderna*, 193 (Jan. 1905), p.153.

The two sexes may be in opposition but men and women are, by the same token, human beings; they have equal rights and it is highly desirable that the legal system take account of that. The key ideas which concern us here are the following: woman is not an incomplete human being and her raison d'être is not limited to her role as mother. Artistic, literary, scientific, and social activity are all compatible with her sex. Consequently, 'a general human education' for women is not only possible but essential.[16]

The Krausists took steps to improve the educational opportunities available to women, and the Revolution of 1868 gave added impetus to this. Scanlon confirms that 'la mayor parte de la iniciativa para reformar la educación de las mujeres durante el último tercio del siglo XIX provino de los krausistas' (*27,* p. 30). Nevertheless, such opportunities were limited, and while considerable reform was effected by Fernando de Castro, newly appointed Rector of the University, the original Krausist philosophy was modified, as he warned women: '¡No mandéis, influíd!'. Although Castro pointed to 'los esfuerzos realizados en otros países para elevar a las mujeres y darles la igualdad con los hombres', he stressed that in Spain the main objective was to 'convencer a la gente de que la mujer tiene que recibir una educación más extensa si se quiere que cumpla su misión en la vida'.[17] Here we note the distinction in motive between the original Krausist aim of individual self-realization *per se*, and Castro's aim to establish the kind of education for women which would most befit 'su misión en la vida', i.e. their role as mothers.[18] As Scanlon stresses, the original Krausists 'no

---

[16] Pierre Jobit, *Les Éducateurs de l'Espagne contemporaine* (Paris: Boccard, 1936), p. 184 (my translation).

[17] Quoted by Yvonne Turín, *La educación y la escuela en España de 1874 a 1902: liberalismo y tradición* (Madrid: Aguilar, 1967), p. 62.

[18] Chris Weedon observes how even today, 'in conservative discourse [...] to be a wife and mother is seen as woman's primary role and the source of self-fulfilment', *Feminist Practice and Poststructuralist Theory* (Oxford: Blackwell, 1987), p. 38.

veían a las mujeres como instrumentos necesarios en el proceso de perfeccionamiento de sus hijos, sino como individuos con un derecho a la educación tanto en beneficio propio como en beneficio de la sociedad' (*27,* p. 7).

Some of those improvements which were made in women's education during the period of the Revolution of 1868 were rescinded by the new Conservative, neo-Catholic Education Minister, Alejandro Pidal, in 1884. Most higher education available to women was directed towards the teaching of children, and the few women admitted to the universities received only *certificados de suficiencia,* rather than official qualifications which would allow them to practise their profession. As Emilia Pardo Bazán was to protest: 'Apenas pueden los hombres formarse idea de lo difícil que es para una mujer adquirir cultura autodidáctica y llenar los claros de su educación [...] Para los varones, todas ventajas, y para la mujer, obstáculos todos' (*24,* p. 13).

Although Pardo Bazán aspired to and achieved a high standard of education through determination and considerable independent means, it is clear that both she and Galdós were disappointed by the decline in progress in women's education towards the end of the century, and each wrote of the superficial veneer of education which had become more fashionable. Pardo Bazán was to stress the need for 'esa educación que Kant llama práctica, la educación de la personalidad, de un ser libre, capaz de bastarse a sí mismo' (*24,* p. 93), and there is little doubt that she would have discussed her views with Galdós at some length.

In 1890, Pardo Bazán founded the magazine *Nuevo Teatro Crítico,* in which she published many of her feminist views, and it was also in this year that she published a series of articles on 'La mujer española'. As Catherine Davies's recent study confirms, she was clearly responding to the rapidly changing social and cultural context and to developments in the women's movement abroad. In 1891 she nominated the early Spanish feminist writer, Concepción Arenal, for the Royal Spanish Academy and, following Arenal's death in 1893, dedicated a lengthy article to her feminist ideas in

Nuevo Teatro Crítico. Pardo Bazán was to become increasingly frustrated by Spain's lack of response to such vital ideas, reaffirmed at the International Conference on the Condition and Rights of Women held in Paris in 1900, which was well attended by delegates from the United States, Mexico, Russia and other countries, but at which she found herself the only Spanish participant.

Catherine Davies concludes that 'Pardo Bazán's main conviction was that women should be educated in order to acquire the rights of men'.[19] This, arguably, was also Tristana's conviction, but such women, in the reality of late-nineteenth and early-twentieth-century Spain, were to be bitterly disappointed. If some who are thus frustrated appear unstable, as does Tristana, Pardo Bazán stresses that 'it is not nature, it is today's society which perhaps unbalances them'.[20]

These women were clearly ready for change, but Spanish society was to resist allowing them much opportunity for change for some time, notwithstanding movements on other fronts. The creation in this novel of the female terms 'médica', 'abogada', 'ministra', etc. were not to be formally accepted into the Spanish language for nearly a century and it is clear that, as Mayoral stresses, Tristana was well ahead of her time (*20*).

John Sinnigen has pointed to the fact that, as the novel was clearly set around 1887–92, Tristana herself must have been born around the time of the Revolution of 1868, and he, among others, finds 'un eco de España en Tristana' (*31*, p. 212). In this national allegory, don Lope is seen as representing the past and 'la aristocracia decadente', Horacio 'la nueva burguesía', and Tristana 'el pueblo'. I find these allegories rather simplistic, but there is clearly something in Sinnigen's conclusion that 'El pueblo y Tristana son los portadores de "la sociedad futura" que los otros no ven'. He relates the history of the social injustice suffered by Tristana to the history of the Revolution and the Restoration (Triste Ana, Triste

---

[19] Catherine Davies, *Spanish Women's Writing 1849–1996* (London: Athlone Press, 1998), pp. 83–86.

[20] Quoted by Catherine Davies, p. 82.

España) which is, nevertheless, 'a punto de ser superada por una nueva expresión de una crisis que, a partir de los años 90, durará, de una forma más o menos abierta u camuflada, según la coyuntura, hasta la Guerra Civil' (*31*, p. 213). Of course, Spanish women's emancipation was to suffer a far greater set-back under Franco after the Civil War, and the equality of opportunity sought by Tristana was not to be formally conceded for nearly a century.

The loss of Cuba in 1898, the last of Spain's once great Empire, gave rise to a national identity crisis which found literary expression in the Generation of '98, who wrote of spiritual anguish and reflected on the past which had led to this sad state. Galdós neither aspired to be nor was considered as a member of the '98 Generation, notwithstanding the national/historical allegories seen in his work by some critics and the clear projection of 'una España nueva' in his contemporary drama. Nevertheless, critics increasingly stress the view that Galdós was ahead of his time: in a recent collection of essays Víctor Fuentes places him at the forefront of the 'regeneracionistas' and Theodore Sackett sees his drama *Bárbara* as based on modernist and 'noventayochista' concerns.[21]

Don Lope's role in *Tristana*, written some six years before the disaster of 1898, is more complex than a mere representation of the decadent aristocracy, if only because he looks further back to the role of the knight-errant, whose values and behaviour he emulates to a certain point and then adapts to suit himself. He can be seen, as suggested at the beginning of this chapter, to reflect nostalgically on the past in his resistance to the current *status quo*, while Tristana can be seen to anticipate the future as a modern-minded woman rather than just a representative of the *pueblo* (of which she is hardly typical anyway). Horacio, for his part, shows apprehension before such modern ideas which at first he seems to embrace but from

---

[21] Víctor Fuentes, 'Galdós en la encrucijada noventayochista: de *Misericordia* a *Electra*' and Theodore Sackett, 'Metadrama, modernismo y noventayochismo en *Bárbara*', in *Realidad e imaginación en la obra de Pérez Galdós,* Rumbos, 13–14 (Neuchâtel: Institut d'Espagnol, Université de Neuchâtel, 1995), pp. 9–23 and 139–51.

which he is soon to flee in order to become part of 'la nueva burguesía', rather than representing it from the beginning. Nevertheless, it is he who recognizes that perhaps Tristana sees the future society 'que nosotros no vemos' (102) and, most probably, do not want to see.

3. Sources and Influences

This novel draws on a wealth of literary, cultural, and biographical sources and influences. The literary and cultural sources have been quite comprehensively outlined and explained by Gordon Minter in the Introduction and Notes to his new edition of the text, so this section will be limited accordingly to those which are arguably the most significant. Nonetheless, it is worth stressing that this text is so rich in artistic allusions as to warrant a full-length study, particularly in view of the fact that, as William H. Shoemaker observes, 'many of the figures and allusions have no specific explanation and are left to the readers' own understanding' (*29*, p. 81). A number of fairly recent studies have explored the multiple levels of possible significance in Galdós's careful use of art and literature in this text.

The enormous range of references includes the work of Cervantes, José Zorrilla, Dante, Velázquez, Lope de Sosa, Baltasar de Alcazar, Mozart, Tirso de Molina, the Duque de Rivas, Calderón de la Barca, Juan Ruiz de Alarcón, Quevedo, Leopardi, Verdi, Fray Luis de León, Quintana, Shakespeare, Rodrigo Caro, Macaulay, Garcilaso de la Vega, Leibnitz, Raphael, Alexandre Dumas *fils*, Beethoven, Apelles, Moreto, Góngora, echoes of *Lazarillo*, citations from biblical sources, and mention of nineteenth-century politicians: Alcalá Galiano, Castelar, and Cánovas.

Literary and Cultural

The weight of literary sources is apparent from the very opening line of *Tristana*, which clearly echoes that of *Don Quijote*: 'En un lugar de la Mancha, de cuyo nombre no quiero acordarme, no ha mucho tiempo que vivía un hidalgo de los de lanza en astillero, adarga antigua, rocín flaco y galgo corredor'. Galdós's narrator begins: 'En el populoso barrio de Chamberí [...] vivía no ha muchos años un hidalgo de buena estampa y nombre peregrino [...]' (1). In each case the hero (or anti-hero) gives himself the chivalric name by which he is known: Cervantes's knight-errant was originally named Quijada or Quesada or Quijada, but he chooses to be called Don Quijote, while Galdós's 'hidalgo' considers the title Don Lope to suit him better than Don Juan López Garrido. They both practise a very particular form of *caballería,* although Don Lope's is more the kind 'que bien podemos llamar sedentaria' (4) rather than *andante.*

Don Lope's ideas are a mixture of logic and *locura,* that Cervantine mix which so fascinated Galdós throughout his career (his first novel was entitled *La sombra* and his last, *La razón de la sinrazón*). Like his famous predecessor, don Lope is also at times forced to confront disillusioning realities, albeit in rather different contexts. Shoemaker points to a number of direct reminiscences of *Don Quijote* in *Tristana*, including don Lope's later recognition of Tristana as 'esta mujer sin par', echoing don Quijote's repeated description of 'la sin par Dulcinea del Toboso' (*29*, p. 84). Indeed, he confirms *Don Quijote* as 'the most enduring and persistent of Galdós' literary recreations which appears in reminiscent linguistic quotations and adaptations, in similar, parallel episodes and situations, in a substratum of *jocoserio* humor and irony, and in deep reincarnations' throughout the writer's work (*29*, p. 208).

Still on the opening page of our novel, the perhaps even greater influence of the ruthlessness of Zorrilla's Don Juan Tenorio is equally apparent, in stark contrast to the chivalry inherited from Don Quijote. Again there is to be a twist as we are given a vision of a Don Juan who is allowed to survive into old age rather than be condemned to the fires of hell. We are told that don Lope is fifty-seven when this story begins, although he will admit to being no older than forty-nine, and that 'se preciaba de haber asaltado más torres de virtud y rendido más plazas de honestidad que pelos tenía en la cabeza'(1). Tristana herself compares her guardian and seducer don Lope directly to Don Juan when she tells her young lover Horacio: 'Sus conquistas son tantas que no se pueden contar. ¡Si tú supieras ...! Aristocracia, clase media, pueblo ..., en todas partes dejó memoria triste, como Don Juan Tenorio'. As in the case of Don Juan, 'no respetó nada, ni la santísima religión ... hasta con monjas y beatas ha tenido amores el maldito' (37). As Minter points out, the *donjuanismo* of Don Lope is apparent in many other ways. When he has to sell his possessions, for example, he clings on to his collection of 'amorous trophies' and similarly, notwithstanding all his conquests, he does not appear to have sired any children, adding to the sense of deliberate parallels with the literary archetype. A further clear parallel can be seen in the naming of Tristana, Doña Ana being the name of the woman Don Juan was pledged to marry. Ironically, of course, don Lope does ultimately marry Tristana, leading Minter to conclude that the archetype of Don Juan grown old 'becomes more of a quixotic figure, a kind of courtly lover paying homage to his lady, a man whose capacity for curiously dignified self-sacrifice may enlist the reader's sympathy' (*22*, p. xiii). I do not see don Lope in quite such romantic terms, but more of this later.

So far as Tristana is concerned, we have already observed that her name, Triste-Ana, can be seen to echo that of Zorilla's Doña Ana. It is also reminiscent of the ill-fated hero of the legend of Tristan and Isolde albeit, interestingly, with a feminized version of the name. Joan Grimbert sees Galdós's *Tristana* as undermining the Tristan legend, notably in Tristana's appropriation of Tristan's attributes and their subsequent subversion (*13*, p. 113). Assuming first Tristan's name and his orphaned state, Tristana aspires to earn her own living and to be her own head of household, refusing to marry Horacio and noting herself that her tastes and abilities make her more like a man than a woman. When her dreams of true independence are shattered, she takes refuge in music, which raises her into another sphere, far beyond the sordid reality of her circumstances. As Horacio listens to her play, he too is transported in a scene reminiscent of Wagner's *Tristan and Isolde*, but as Grimbert points out, in Galdós's novel Tristana and Horacio accede to a spiritual realm in which they are in no way united; rather, each revels separately in a state of complete and absolute isolation. In this way music, so important throughout the Tristan legend, actually presides in the novel over the final phase of a failed love relationship. Grimbert concludes that while Tristana's constant refusal to marry Horacio and her initial determination to embrace a career show that her ideal transcends the masculine/feminine dichotomy, her eventual acquiescence in marriage to don Lope demonstrates the abysmal failure of that ideal (*13*, p. 118).

Yet although she is ultimately to be a sad victim (of Society? of Nature?) as are so many of the heroines of Galdós's novels up to this point, Tristana also assumes for herself and is given by the narrator various alternative literary and cultural identities, the implications of which will be explored presently. Such identities range from the narrator's early description of Tristana as a passive 'dama japonesa' to her own identification with the role of the assertive Lady Macbeth as she cries 'Unsex me here!' (67), in her desire to assume the strength and freedom of the male.

From the beginning, many of the numerous artistic references are from Italian sources, notably the *Divina commedia* of Dante, the verse of Leopardi, and the libretti of various operas. In the early description of Tristana as an immaculate and impassive Japanese *dama*, for example, the narrator tells us her countenance appeared to proclaim to the world: '*la vostra miseria non me tange*' (3), yet later there is deep irony in her own quoting from Dante in a letter to Horacio: '*E se non piangi, de che pianger suoli?*' ['And if you weep not, at what do you ever weep?'] (67, translated by Minter), as her destiny is about to be determined and her ambitions definitively crushed. Her lighthearted reference to the tragic Violetta in Verdi's *La Traviata* is, of course, to prove equally ironic.

The fact that Tristana is so isolated from society naturally fuels her increasingly active mind's dependence on the fictional and the imaginary, a tendency reinforced by those to whom she is close: her mother, doña Josefina, with her penchant for romantic novels; don Lope in his attempts to romanticize the ugly truth of his seduction of her; and Horacio, with whom she enacts so many literary games. Even the maid Saturna, ostensibly the realist, unwittingly encourages this reliance on the fictional by causing Tristana to realize that the only honourable profession open to her is in the theatre, leading her subsequently to quote Shakespeare again: 'All the world's a stage' (65). This tendency is increased still further by the lovers' enforced separation and the creative nature of their amorous correspondence, which has been carefully analysed by Gonzalo Sobejano (*33*).

A number of the references to Dante's *Divina commedia* — Count Ugolini imprisoned in a tower and Francesca da Rimini killed for her infidelity — serve to underline both Tristana's entrapment with don Lope and her doomed romance with Horacio. Don Lope's sexual jealousy is also parallelled with examples from Spanish Golden Age drama, and correspondingly he threatens his ward: 'Si te sorprendo en algún mal paso, te mato, cree que te mato' (18).

As Shoemaker has illustrated at some length, cultural reminiscences enrich the portrayal of Horacio on several levels, from the description of his fierce, avaricious grandfather as belonging to 'la escuela del licenciado Cabra', a clear reference to Quevedo's *El Buscón*, to Horacio's own likening of don Lope to 'una figura escapada del Cuadro de las Lanzas' by Velázquez, and biblical and mythical references both reflecting and anticipating aspects of the young couple's relationship. Even Saturna is seen as somewhat reminiscent of the fifteenth-century procuress Celestina, and doña Josefina's momentary lucidity just before her death is directly linked in the text to that of 'don Quijote moribundo' (*29*, pp. 84–85).

Galdós's use of the imagination, both artistic — writing, painting or musical performance — and religious, as a central constituent in inter-personal relationships in this novel has recently been explored by Eric Southworth. He stresses that such imagination is involved in the creation of value, meaning, and purpose in life: philosophers suspicious of the supernatural had already begun to think of religious belief as a human creation, as an aesthetic response to the human predicament (*33*).

Religious references to Tristana increase towards the end of the novel, notably allusions to St Cecilia, the patron saint of music and musicians. As Minter points out, St Cecilia not only converts her husband to Christianity, but inspires him to respect her virginity within marriage. He also stresses the reference to Beatrice from the *Divina commedia* and speculates that the theme of the *camino de perfección* to which she is connected might also be applicable to *Tristana*, giving the novel a religious dimension with a satisfactory outcome (*22,* p. xiv). This is an interesting interpretation, although it is not one which convinces me. Nevertheless, it is clear that the wealth of allusion greatly broadens the possibilities in this text.

It is equally clear that don Lope actively compounds Tristana's troubles, encouraging in her 'la fácil disposición para idealizar las cosas, para verlo todo como no es' (12). He himself is ironically portrayed as the perpetuator of values enshrined in the classics of Spain's Golden Age, reinforced with the image of Velázquez's *La rendición de Breda*, and Southworth points out how 'in all this, Galdós is joining in existing nineteenth-century debates on Spain's artistic classics as vehicles of the national spirit, for good as well as ill' (*34*). He shows how the novel further explores the relative merits of idealizing and a realist art, another area of nineteenth-century polemic, relating to which kind is the more Spanish. Tristana's participation in her imagination in art (Velázquez's *Las hilanderas*) and music (Beethoven's sonata) as she is sedated with chloroform prior to the amputation of her leg is particularly poignant, as she strives for perfection. Yet Peter Bly's view that she uses art as a substitute for living is perhaps a little extreme and simplistic: 'Tristana's strong imagination is depraved by her discovery of the world of art. She has to be brought back to reality by the violent shock of her amputation.'[22] Indeed, it seems to me that it is following the amputation that Tristana most clearly and deliberately distances herself from reality.

For Bly, it is 'the vulnerability of the human eye to the attractions of the visual arts' which 'becomes the main matter of Galdós' fiction' (p. 211). While art, and Horacio's profession as a painter, clearly play key roles in this complex text, however, in my view they constitute a vital part rather than the 'main matter'. Bly further concludes that through the sale of don Lope's art objects, 'Art becomes the means, however indirectly and unwittingly it is engineered, by which the subservience of Tristana to her eventual guardian and lover is assured' (p. 212) and, again, I see this as a contributory rather than primary factor. At the same time, as Bly

---

[22] Peter Bly, *Vision and the Visual Arts in Galdós* (Liverpool: Francis Cairns, 1986), p. 218.

clearly illustrates, various threads of visual art material — paintings, picturesque landscapes, art metaphors and a discussion of the value of eyesight — are all filtered directly into Horacio's love affair with Tristana, which he describes as 'the main story'. Yet while such material is clearly of great value and brilliantly woven into the tale, just as the young couple's love affair is of considerable significance, I believe there is more to the novel than this and that the affair alone does not constitute the main story.

Similarly, where I depart from Noel Valis's penetrating study on this theme is in her statement that 'significantly, the only way Tristana can conceive of herself is as an artist, whether as painter, musician, or actress. Anything else, anything less than this artistic ideal leaves her utterly indifferent' (*37*, p. 212). Yet at the beginning when Tristana ponders on her future and her ideal of independence, the first potential careers she considers (which are not open to her as a woman) are not artistic ones. When Saturna effectively tells her that the only honourable profession open to her is acting, Tristana responds 'la seguiría yo si tuviera facultades; pero me parece que no las tengo'. She immediately goes on to say: 'Si nos hicieran médicas, abogadas, siquiera boticarias o escribanas, ya que no ministras y senadoras, vamos, podríamos ...' (14). But of course, in nineteenth-century Spain, women *no pueden* because the opportunities are not open to them. Nevertheless, Tristana believes that she is capable of practising those professions open only to men, insisting 'hasta para eso del Gobierno y la política me parece a mí que había de servir yo' (15). Just as she states at the outset that she does not think she is ideally suited to theatrical work, so in the same breath Tristana also declares 'No valgo, no, para encerronas de toda la vida' (14). In the 'real world' of the novel, however, as Saturna points out, there are few alternatives open to her other than enclosure in marriage or the convent, possibly a career on the stage, or 'lo otro'. Tristana then moves on to the thought of earning a living through painting or writing, acknowledging that she lacks training but not ideas. And indeed, opportunities to practise the arts are, in limited fashion, accorded to her, although with little advice or information available to help her utilize her talent in the quest for independence. She subsequently, as Valis suggests, uses art (which is accessible to her) as 'an instrument subordinate to her quest for self-knowledge, for self-awareness'. It is predominantly through art, in the absence of any other means, that Tristana will attempt to find herself, but as Valis goes on to ask: 'The question is, though, does she?' (*37*, p. 208).

Tristana's allusions to Shakespeare, as when she quotes 'To be or not to be', are seen by Southworth 'to encapsulate central aspects of her existential predicament, and are a graphic way of conveying the deeper confusion in her life' (*34*). This critic does not seem to be any more convinced either by the notion of Tristana as purely 'an emblem of the bad artist, who uses Art as a substitute for living', or of her final religious conversion than I am.

It is only after the amputation of her leg, when Tristana acknowledges: 'Soy otra', that she appears deliberately to distance herself from the 'reality' of the text that will not allow her to find her true self and develop an identity of her own. At first it seems that music helps her to disengage herself from the world around her or, as Southworth suggests, it may be 'the only fitting form of self-expression left to this unhappy woman' (*34*). But then she turns to religion in her search for some form of goal or ideal, previously projected onto her own re-creation of Horacio (increasingly idealized as her illness progressed) and now 'Si antes era un hombre, luego fue Dios'. We are also told that 'la contemplación mental del ídolo érale más fácil en la iglesia que fuera de ella, las formas plásticas del culto la ayudaban a sentirlo' (109). The original manuscript continued here, adding 'y cultivarlo', but these words were subsequently deleted by Galdós, as if he did not wish to give the idea that this feeling was developed into anything deeper. Southworth observes that some readers have seen Tristana's earlier idealizations of a human being as a step on her path to God, but points to the use of the word 'ídolo' and the 'formas plásticas del culto' as suggesting a rather superficial adherence to form and idea ('¿sólo exterior?' the narrator suggests) rather than firm doctrinal conviction. Tristana's emotional restlessness is also ironically suggested by the narrator as he tells us that she 'llegó a olvidarse del primer aspecto de su ideal [changed by Galdós at the last minute in the galley proofs from 'ídolo'], y no vio al fin más que el segundo, que era seguramente el definitivo'(109). 'Seguramente'? Maybe ...

Biographical

While reference to biography can frequently appear speculative, irrelevant, at best unfashionable and at worst even misleading, biography is so patently a source in this novel that to ignore it is arguably to lose a significant dimension of the work. This is so not only because the creation of the protagonist and her dilemma were prompted by a particular woman in the author's life, but because important sections of the text were originally penned by her. I refer to the young actress Concha-Ruth Morell with whom Galdós had been having an affair and whose letters to him were, as she herself indignantly exclaimed, 'literalmente copiadas' in the novel.

Indeed, where the vast majority of Galdosian heroines are avid readers, Tristana is one of the few who is given an authorial role. The significance of this act of writing is stressed in the text by the reference to the protagonist as 'una hoja de papel blanco' (3), upon which she is arguably to attempt 'to write herself'.

Notwithstanding her later indignation at Galdós's use of her personal letters, Concha-Ruth was naturally eager to read 'esa novela que dices que he inspirado yo' (*32*, p.105). The 310 letters conserved in the Casa-Museo Pérez Galdós attest the significance of her role in this text on several levels. A number of these letters have now been published, and direct parallels with a number of those reproduced in the novel established. It is clear there were many parallels between Concha-Ruth and Tristana, including their background, their orphaned state, their seduction by their guardian, their plans for acting as their only means of achieving honourable independence (although it was a profession neither of them felt particularly suited to), and also what Lambert describes as their 'entusiasmos locos y sus desalientos' (*18*, p. 42). Much of their ambition and frustration is reflected through their letters, Concha-Ruth declaring in a letter to Galdós:

Me he empeñado en un imposible. Quiero tener una
profesión y no sirvo para nada, bien claro está. No sé
hacer más que amar, pero el amor no es un oficio ... (*32*,
p. 100)

In like manner, Tristana is to write to Horacio:

¿Será verdad, Dios mío, que pretendo un imposible?
Quiero tener una profesión, y no sirvo para nada, ni sé
nada de cosa alguna. Esto es horrendo. (61)

They are equally frustrated by their at times conflicting passion for
independence and for love and Concha-Ruth, having read the novel,
writes to Galdós: '¿Me quedaré en la estacada como Tristana? Tal
vez, pero mi *pata* es el corazón' (*32*, p. 108).

Benito Madariaga points to the similarity in appearance of the
real and the fictional woman, each being 'atractiva, esbelta,
ingeniosa y "de una blancura casi inverosímil de puro alabastrina"'
(*19*, p. 83). Indeed, the likeness extends still further. When I was first
studying Concha-Ruth's letters in Las Palmas back in the eighties
and struggling to read some of the photocopied sheets, I was allowed
access to a few of the original letters.[23] One of these was still in its
envelope, within which I found, carefully wrapped in a piece of
tissue paper, a lock of Concha-Ruth's long, fine, silky, chestnut-
coloured hair, exactly corresponding to the description of Tristana's:
'castaño el cabello y no muy copioso, brillante como torzales de
seda' (2).

A few of Concha-Ruth's letters are signed 'Tristóna' (I have
reproduced one in *9*, Appendix 2) and there are some parallels with
Tristan and Isolde, as indicated earlier, albeit with a twist. Indeed,
parallels can be seen in the triangle Tristana, don Lope, and Horacio,
the triangle Concha-Ruth, Galdós, and the older man in her life she
called 'papá', and the triangle Tristan, Isolde, and King Mark. The
twist lies in the fact that it is Horacio's character which corresponds
to Tristan rather than Tristana's, although, like don Lope, the King

---

[23] Casa-Museo Pérez Galdós, Caja 10, Carp. 37–38, Leg. 105.

will separate the young lovers. In the case of the real-life triangle, of course, Galdós is not exactly a 'young lover', being well into his forties at the time of his affair with Concha-Ruth, although he is clearly younger than her so-called 'papá'.

From the evidence available, it seems probable that Galdós's relationship with Concha-Ruth began in the summer of 1891, after his love affair with Emilia Pardo Bazán had ended and after the birth of his daughter María by Lorenza Cobián in January of that year. It is apparent that their affair continued, off and on, for some years, Benito Madariaga's recent study confirming that they spent time together in Paris, Navarre, and, as late as 1898, in Santander, and that their subsequent break-up caused great upset and subsequently, even scandal.[24] Nevertheless, it seems that despite her misfortunes, her illness, and financial problems, Concha-Ruth clung to her increasingly radical socialist and feminist ideals. On 23 June 1904 she gave a talk at a meeting of the Federal Republicans in Santander, subsequently published in the local press, which 'trata de un alegato feminista donde la autora se declara antirreligiosa, anti-belicista, republicana y anarquista, y termina con el grito: ¡Viva la República Federal, precursora de la Anarquía!' (*19*, p. 81). Not for Concha-Ruth the final passive indifference of Tristana.

It was Concha-Ruth who was to play the role of Clotilde in the dramatization of *Realidad*, wherein Galdós initiates the exploration of a viable alternative role for women in society, initially considered in more radical terms in *Tristana*. The fact that, rather than condensing this role in the adaptation of the dialogue novel *Realidad* for the stage, Galdós reworked and greatly expanded the role of Clotilde, who has been seen as the precursor to his concept of 'la mujer nueva', is witness to the importance he attributed to it. Having confronted the problems of radical feminism in nineteenth-century Spain in his writing of *Tristana*, clearly influenced by Concha-Ruth Morell, Galdós appears to have broken through some of the reservations he previously held concerning the possibility of a new

---

[24] Benito Madariaga, 'Concepción Morell en la vida y obra de Galdós', *Altazor* (Santander), 1 (1992), 63–73.

role for women in society, as he proceeds to portray this on stage through his contemporary drama.

While the influence of Concha-Ruth on Galdós's literary output may be considered by some critics to be irrelevant, there can be no denying that it was her pen which wrote some of the crucial lines in Tristana, and for that she must be acknowledged.

4. Style, Imagery, and Narrative Stance

Hazel Gold's recent study on 'The Reframing of Realism' includes *Tristana* in the group of Galdós's novels traditionally held in lesser esteem because they violate the principles of unity and closure that have typically framed discussion of the realist novel.[25] Such novels, which include *La incógnita* and *Realidad*, have enjoyed closer scrutiny of late. In contrast to the conclusions of earlier critics, for example, Farris Anderson considers *Tristana* to be 'a coherent novel and, paradoxically, a complete novel, if by "completeness" we understand compliance with aesthetic principles established within the work rather than with expectations that are externally imposed' (*2*, p. 62).

As indicated earlier, by the time of penning *Tristana* Galdós had already fully exploited the potential of the realist novel, notably with his masterpiece *Fortunata y Jacinta*, and was clearly in experimental mode. So while *Tristana* still falls within the category of nineteenth-century realism, it does not quite conform to our expectations of the genre. This is perhaps most apparent in the style and presentation of the novel.

Style

Tristana is less expansive than the majority of Galdós's *novelas contemporáneas* in terms of its depiction of society and settings. It is a novel which is very enclosed in terms of space, and with reason because, of course, it focuses on the confinement of the protagonist, primarily in terms of movement and identity. It focuses less on external movements and settings, more on interior settings and

---

[25] Hazel Gold, *The Reframing of Realism: Galdós and the Discourses of the Nineteenth-Century Spanish Novel* (Durham, NC: Duke University Press, 1993), p. 185.

psychology. Instead of the vast number of brilliantly portrayed secondary characters we have become accustomed to encountering in a Galdós novel, all interacting within a vividly portrayed dynamic society, we are confined to the relatively static close quarters of a handful of characters virtually isolated from society, whose situation is presented with more than a dash of irony.

This irony is apparent from the opening page of the novel, as is the richness of the language and the wealth of artistic allusions. The grandiose style of the first chapter is, of course, a parody of the misguided grandeur of Cervantes's hero, don Quijote, as Galdós's narrator slyly mocks our *hidalgo*, don Lope. But the narrator, as we shall see, is himself a particularly slippery character, forcing the reader to read with care.

While the psychology is complex, the action is simple and the construction tight, leading Shoemaker to conclude that the novel is 'technically among the best of Galdós' novels, if not the very best of all' (*29*, p. 76). This is interesting, particularly as Pardo Bazán had insisted a century earlier that, had the theme of the work been more satisfactorily resolved, *Tristana* could have been 'la mejor novela de Galdós' (*24*, p. 137). We shall shortly return to what many consider to be the main theme of the novel.

Detailed study of the structure of *Tristana* has been carried out by Vernon Chamberlin (*7*), Germán Gullón (*14*) and, more recently, Chad Wright (*40*). Chamberlin likens the form of *Tristana* to that of a sonata. In a number of studies, he has expounded the hypothesis of a musical structure pertaining both to *Fortunata y Jacinta* and (more effectively in my view) to *Tristana*, recently stressing his view that such structure governs the resolution of these two works. He points out that Galdós explained that he had been influenced by 'la composición beethoviana' in the creation of his play of 1902, *Alma y vida*, and that, towards the end of *Tristana*, the organ-playing protagonist specifically says that she is playing Beethoven sonatas.

The sonata form can be seen reflected in the structure of this novel by tracing analogues of the two main competing themes of the first movement of a typical sonata. Chamberlin sees the two main competing themes of the novel as being the penchant for domination and the contrasting desire for independence and self-fulfilment and what he describes as the 'harmonic resolution' of the novel as reflecting the 'coda' of the sonata. While impressed by his exposition of a musical structure in this novel, however, I am less convinced by his recent conclusion that 'artistic considerations are given preference over any sociological statement'.[26]

Germán Gullón focuses on the traditional love triangle formed by Tristana, don Lope and Horacio, superimposing on this the corresponding 'arquetipos míticos' which 'les vienen grandes y por contraste con ellos los tres entes ficticios resultan un tanto ridículos y patéticos'. He concludes that '*Tristana*, debido a su consistente estructura novelesca, permeada por referencias literarias de diversas épocas, no puede ocupar el puesto que con frecuencia se le asigna, el de un alegato de un feminismo incipiente' (*14*, p. 27). In my view, however, 'la profunda literaturización de la obra' further underlines the irony inherent in the text and does not negate the feminist theme.

More recently, Chad Wright has stressed the circular structure of *Tristana*, the circle being 'both the shape of the narrative (a misshapen circle, of course)' and representing 'its meaning: the end takes us back to the beginning'. He sees Tristana's story as 'a quest for being, but told ironically' (*40*). He illustrates how the circle, as a sign, is multivalent and ambiguous in this text and, furthermore, how the novel is sustained to a large degree by circles of repetitions. Wright's perceptive study concludes that 'even the use of "puntos suspensivos" is ironic: the device does not bring the sentence to a full stop, but rather keeps the sentence open and incomplete by repeating itself' (*40*).

Galdós's use of language in *Tristana* is, as ever, extraordinarily dextrous, and the significance of the form and nature of language consciously highlighted in the text, as Erna Pfeiffer has recently illustrated (*26*). For Gonzalo Sobejano, 'los capítulos XIV a XXI de *Tristana* constituyen un ejercicio de penetración en la realidad del lenguaje amoroso no llevado hasta ese límite por ningún

---

[26] Vernon Chamberlin, 'The So-Called Problem of Closure in Two Galdosian Novels Revisited via Musical Structure', unpublished paper given at the 1998 Modern Language Association Convention in San Francisco.

novelista español del siglo XIX ni por Galdós mismo en otra de sus novelas' (*33,* p. 86). He points out how 'el vocabulario de los amantes mezcla locuciones chocarreras con palabras de otro idioma; usa formas de lenguaje sugeridas or anécdotas, chascarrillos, pasajes graves y versos célebres; pone motes en lugar de nombres; sazona el diálogo con terminachos grotescos y con expresiones líricas'. Furthermore, he shows such language to be 'en perpetuo trance de renovación' (*33,* p. 86). Early in the novel, of course, we are told how Tristana learns to 'valerse de las ductilidades de la palabra' (13); it is her voice which takes over the central part of the novel, but which is totally withdrawn at the end.

Although, as observed, the plot is simple, it is not simply told, neither are the main characters straightforward or static. The question of identity is an overriding one from the start, with the slippery description of don Lope, although it is to become most contentious in the case of Tristana. The quest for both autonomous identity and love is to become ever more intense as the two become paradoxically interdependent and incompatible. Finally, the psychological and sociological struggle is compounded by physical disaster in the form of a *deus ex machina*.

Just as Máximo Manso becomes flesh and blood on the pages of *El amigo Manso*, 'convertido en carne mortal', and tells us 'El dolor me dijo que yo era un hombre' (*OC, NI,* 1186), so. Tristana, who also starts as a blank page, assumes the 'sangre y médula de mujer' (13), rejecting the role of *muñeca*.[27] In this sense, it seems, both protagonists have some control over their creation, just as ultimately, both will choose to withdraw from the 'reality' of their text. In *Tristana*, the numerous literary allusions (from both 'la alta literatura' and the popular) invariably play a part in the identity quest, as the protagonist seeks an autonomy of her own. While she aligns herself with many female figures, it is clear she does not want to assume a traditionally feminine role, as she insists 'Me parezco a los hombres' (48) and demands the same opportunities.

---

[27] B. Pérez Galdós, *Obras completas, Novelas I*, p. 1186. Henceforth this form of abbreviation will be used in the text for other works by Galdós.

Tristana progressively takes control from the narrator and asserts her own voice, notably through the lengthy epistolary section, only to lose it totally at the end of the text. She first voices her desires and ambitions to Saturna, who tries to make her face the reality of nineteenth-century Spanish society, insisting 'para eso hay que ser hombre, señorita ...' (15). But Tristana will not give in so easily, seeing herself potentially capable of practising professions from which women were excluded, but for which she created female equivalents: 'médica', 'abogada', etc. (14).

Tristana was to discuss her ideas with Horacio and explore them in greater depth and detail through the many letters which constitute the central part of the novel. The passion and desire expressed in these letters, so often contradictory and confused in their intensity, is reminiscent of the letters from Heloise to Abelard, which in turn have frequently been compared to Guilleragues's famous *Letters of a Portuguese Nun*. Indeed, there are many links and potentially fruitful points of comparison between both these earlier texts and the letters found in *Tristana*.[28]

Like Tristana, albeit many centuries earlier, Heloise was passionately in love but argued against marriage. Ironically, while the amputation of Tristana's leg has been seen by a number of critics as the 'castration' which, as well as further constraining her, led to Horacio's loss of desire for her, it is Abelard who is literally castrated.[29] Heloise blames this castration for his loss of desire and interest in her as she writes: 'It was desire, not affection, which bound you to me, the flames of lust rather than love'.[30] Similarly, in *The Letters of a Portuguese Nun*, Mariana, a nun seduced and abandoned by an officer in the French forces which occupied Portugal in the 1660s, writes to him: 'I know neither who I am, nor what I am doing, nor what I want. I am torn by a thousand conflicting feelings. Can anyone imagine a more deplorable

---

[28] See, for example, Hazel Gold's study, 'Cartas de mujeres y la mediación epistolar en *Tristana*' *(13)*.

[29] On the amputation, see especially Bridget Aldaraca (*1*, p. 244).

[30] *The Letters of Abelard and Heloise*, trans. by Betty Radice (Harmondsworth: Penguin, 1974), p. 116.

state?'.[31] Peggy Kamuf's study of feminine desire links this state to the hysteria that Freud concluded invariably sprang from a story of seduction or even rape by the father, or a fatherlike figure, although in 1897 he modified this theory, suspecting that the memory of the specific event was frequently masked by several layers of fantasy (p. 47). Mariana, like Tristana, finally stops writing, and Louise Horowitz explains: 'There is no other way out except to stop writing [...] Mariana's final decision, to stop writing, is truly the only authentic one [...] Her repression is thus total'.[32] There is not the space here to pursue these links, but they illustrate the psychological complexities which can be explored through the use of such epistolary dialogue.

The multiple voices and identities assumed by Tristana in her letters further reflect her intense, increasingly desperate hunger for knowledge and power, so often linked by feminists. The power she seeks is predominantly over her own destiny, described by Hélène Cixous as the form of 'woman's powers', rather than over others, notwithstanding her desire for equality of opportunity with men.[33] The power and control Tristana wields with her pen and the fluctuating balance between the potentially 'real' and the fictional or metafictional identities she assumes become increasingly unstable as her illness progresses, the telling moment being when she finally drops her pen and returns to the state of the *muñeca*. This movement foreshadows the definitive withdrawal of her voice from the text, as she hands the pen over to don Lope.

The irony which pervades this ambiguous text, from the parody in its opening page to the closing words of its arguably bitter end, is a key feature of the novel's style and so sophisticated is its use that it keeps any hope of a definitive interpretation just out of our grasp.

---

[31] Quoted by Peggy Kamuf, *Fictions of Feminine Desire: Disclosures of Heloise* (Lincoln: University of Nebraska Press, 1982), p. 48.

[32] Louise Horowitz, *Love and Language: A Study of the Classical French Moralist Writers* (Columbus: Ohio State University Press, 1977), p. 142.

[33] Hélène Cixous, 'Entretien avec Françoise van Rossum-Guyon', *Revue des Sciences Humaines*, 168 (Oct.–Dec. 1977), 483–84.

Imagery

The imagery in this novel is highly provocative, particularly in feminist terms.

The protagonist is not presented to us at the beginning of her tale as an individual human being with a name, but rather as an object, a possession, a plaything. And because she is a passive object rather than an individual human being, she appears at first resigned to always being 'una petaca', 'una posesión', and ultimately, 'una muñeca'. The first chapter of the novel closes with the description of Tristana's relatonship to don Lope: 'no era nada y lo era todo, pues le pertenecía como una petaca, un mueble o una prenda de ropa, sin que nadie se la pudiera disputar; ¡y ella parecía tan resignada a ser petaca, y siempre petaca!' (p. 3). Jennifer Lowe quotes the second definition of 'petaca' in the *Diccionario de la Real Academia Española* as: 'estuche de cuero, metal u otra materia que sirve para llevar cigarros o tabaco picado'. She points to the number of references in the text to don Lope's cigar and observes: 'The coexistence of Lope's cigar and Tristana as his 'petaca' needs no elaboration', further linking his control over the terms of their relationship with his wish to hold or relinquish his cigar.[34] An example of this occurs when he suspects her of slipping out of his grasp, and warns her: '— Mucho cuidado, niña — dijo el caballero, dando una feroz mordida al cigarro de estanco que fumaba (por no poder gastar otros) que fumaba.' (39). The cigar continues to be regarded a symbol of male power, as recently stressed by Bonnie Greer: 'A man smoking a big, fat cigar is, for most of us, a symbol of power and potency. We take for granted that the cigar is the image of the hard man, one of the definitive phallic symbols'.[35] It is, perhaps, a little ironic that here don Lope is able to afford only a cheap 'cigarro de estanco'.

---

[34] Jennifer Lowe, 'Cigars, Slippers and Nightcaps: Attitudes and Actions in *La Regenta* and *Tristana*', *Anales Galdosianos*, 27–28 (1992–93), 125–29, pp. 125 and 127.

[35] Bonnie Greer, 'How a stogie changed my life', *The Guardian*, 17 August, 1999, p. 5.

The image of the doll is, of course, a famous one, made the more so through Ibsen's classic work·. Galdós himself had used the image frequently in his novels, notably in *Fortunata y Jacinta,* where Fortunata, having been so manipulated by society, 'figurábase ser una muñeca viva' (*OC, NII,*709). This image, however, is one which Tristana, on what appears to be her awakening, is anxious to shake off completely, and she assumes life as a woman of flesh and blood, declaring 'Aquí estoy' as she discards 'la estopa de la muñeca' (13).

With this apparent re-birth, Tristana is described as acquiring wings: another image used by Galdós with some frequency and considerable significance from as early as *Gloria* (see *9,* Chapter 2). Wings can clearly be seen to symbolize the capacity for movement and freedom although, perhaps ironically, they are also attached to angels, and the 'ángel del hogar' is a quite different image altogether, more aligned to that of the *muñeca*. The crucial factor here is whether the wings are clipped or allowed to spread. This point is made very clearly by Galdós from his early novels to his later contemporary drama and crystallized in *Tristana.* Indeed, in this novel it is brutally reinforced through the amputation of the heroine's leg, forcing her to conform to the famous Spanish proverb: 'La mujer honrada, pierna quebrada y en casa.'

Much has been written recently on the significance of the amputated leg in this novel. Earlier critics tended to dismiss this rather melodramatic turn of events as a *deus ex machina*: a way of resolving what appeared to be an insoluble dilemma. But it is arguably more than this. The whole notion of mutilation is a pertinent one, as implied by the Spanish proverb quoted above and stressed by the contemporary feminist, Concepción Arenal, who wrote in 1883 of how society 'ha querido limitar la vida de la mujer, física, moral e intelectual, de manera que no saliese del hogar doméstico, sin ver que no era obra de concentración sino de mutilación la que se hacía'.[36]

Images of mutilation are evident from the beginning of the novel, indicating an incapacity to function properly. Don Lope's

---

[36] Concepción Arenal, *La mujer de su casa* (Madrid: Gras y Compañía, 1883), p. 88.

moral sense, for example, is described as 'cual órgano que ha sufrido una mutilación y sólo funciona con limitaciones' (10). Tristana first meets Horacio against a background of deaf-mute and blind children, whose 'ojos vacíos [...] insensibles a la luz' (20) can be seen to foreshadow the denial of light to Tristana, who repeatedly insists: 'Quiero luz, más luz, siempre más luz' (71). Light, as an image of knowledge and awareness, is used frequently by Galdós, and its significance is stressed by Pardo Bazán as she quotes Legouvé's insistence: '¡Apartemos vanas objeciones inspiradas en leyes de un día: en nombre de la eternidad, debéis a la mujer la luz!' (*24*, p. 93).

Ultimately, both Horacio and don Lope want 'aves domésticas' (103) of both the feathered and the human variety, confined to barracks, while Tristana wants to spread her wings. But our heroine's wings are to be definitively clipped, for 'su destino [...] no le permite revoloteos ni correrías' (87). Following her operation, 'denegaba su propio ser' and 'ni una vez siquiera pensó en escribir cartas' (90). Hence her sense of identity is clearly linked to her use of the word and, symbolically, the power of the pen which she has relinquished. As she reverts to the role of the passive *muñeca*, we are told this change has occurred 'sin duda, por efecto de una metamorfosis verificada en su alma después de la mutilación de su cuerpo' (104). The few words uttered or written by Tristana after the amputation confirm this: 'Soy otra' she declares, and writes briefly to Horacio: 'Ya Tristana no es lo que fue' (91).

In Chad Wright's recent study of 'corporal fragmentation' in *Tristana*, he explains that the body has its own discourse and points to the way torture is usually inflicted to silence the 'voice' of the victim by destruction of the body (*39*, p. 140). He stresses the fact that most critics have overlooked Galdós's preoccupation with the body and his particular fascination with its fragmented form as well as the confinement of the female form. With the fragmentation of Tristana's body comes the fragmentation of her discourse: she can no longer write and tells don Lope, 'No se me ocurre nada' (90).

The amputation itself is one of the most naturalistic sections of the novel, and has been interpreted variously. Sinnigen stresses the phallic symbolism of the amputated leg, that 'objeto largo y estrecho envuelto en una sábana' (89), which he and a number of other critics see as a kind of symbolic castration for Tristana (*30*, pp. 56–57). Minter, on the other hand, argues that as castration normally entails removal of the testicles, then the symbolism is not so clear, and he sees a more likely analogy with the removal of Christ's body to the sepulchre prior to his resurrection (*22*, p. xviii). But, of course, Christ was not believed to have been resurrected in a mutilated form. The text does make it very clear that after the amputation and her marriage to don Lope, Tristana is both silent and indifferent and I see little evidence for the argument that 'far from being symbolically castrated, Tristana, when she recovers from the operation, figuratively starts to wear the trousers' (p. xix). In my reading of the conclusion of the novel, she is confined to 'la maldita enagua' and the kitchen sink as she exclaims '¿Qué remedio tengo más que conformarme?' (104). Once again, however, the possibility of such varied readings illustrates the sophisticated and slippery nature of the text.

The image of 'la maldita enagua' (15) is one of several images of female confinement found in this novel which can also be seen to link the body with the soul or spirit. Galdós makes this link very clear in *Realidad*, the play that was his dramatic début in the year of *Tristana*, where the heroine Augusta recoils against 'este inmenso hastío de la buena sociedad, de esa educación meticulosa y puritana, que nos desfigura el alma, como el maldito corsé nos desfigura el cuerpo'.[37]

Narrative Stance

The narrator in this novel appears particularly and deliberately elusive, as if he were actively playing with the reader, first one way and then the other, misleading and confusing as he goes. At first he presents himself as an unnamed acquaintance — the clearly unreliable narrator often used by Galdós in the *novelas contemporáneas* — referring to 'la primera vez que tuve conocimiento de

---

[37] *El teatro de Galdós: 'Realidad' (1892)*, ed. Lisa P. Condé (Lewiston, NY: Mellen Press, 1993), p. 28.

tal personaje' (1). But then he goes on to give us information most
unlikely to be known by a mere acquaintance: don Lope's real age.
As Catherine Jagoe points out, the other major level of ambiguity in
the narrator's technique is to oscillate constantly between complicity
with and criticism of the characters (*16*, pp. 127–28).

The narrator's description of don Lope is very clearly tongue-
in-cheek, and we very soon become aware of the irony invariably
underlying narratorial comment. His description of Tristana at first
appears more sympathetic, although again we notice the constant
slippage between omniscient and eyewitness observer in terms of
factual information. Seymour Chatman's study of narrative structure
in fiction and film stresses the need to distinguish between narrative
voice and point of view, defining the former as 'the speech or other
overt means through which events and existents are communicated'
and the latter as 'physical place or ideological situation or practical
life-orientation to which narrative events stand in relation'.[38]

In the first part of the novel, the narrator appears to adopt an
anti-patriarchal stance, as Tristana is presented as 'cautiva',
'esclava', and don Lope 'su dueño' and 'amo'. But then, of course,
don Lope had seduced his young ward, which behaviour could
hardly be condoned, notwithstanding Nimetz's description of him as
'a wonderful old rake'.[39] From the time of Tristana's intensely
passionate affair with Horacio, however, the narrator does appear to
distance himself more from her and, according to Jagoe, 'attention is
largely focused on the reactions and thought processes of the two
male protagonists and the male narrator, as they react to Tristana'
(*16*, p. 132).

Jagoe considers that the narrative ambivalence towards
Tristana might be explained by 'the incipient negativity towards
Morell that was to lead Galdós to distance himself from her' (*16,* p.
133). While the novel was clearly inspired by Concha-Ruth,
however, it is my view that the question is more complex than this

---

[38] Seymour B. Chatman, *Story and Discourse: Narrative Structure in
Fiction and Film* (Ithaca: Cornell University Press, 1978), p. 153.

[39] Michael Nimetz, *Humour in Galdós* (New Haven: Yale University Press,
1968), p. 91.

and, of course, author and narrator are not one and the same person. Furthermore, had Concha-Ruth served to convince Galdós of the justification of the proverb 'Mujer honrada: pierna quebrada y en casa', he would not have immediately proceeded to develop his concept of 'la mujer nueva' on stage where, far from being restrained, wings clipped, his new heroine takes control and society is advised, '¡No le cortéis las alas, y veréis hasta dónde se remonta!' (*OC, CTC, 382*).[40]

Nevertheless, we are left in *Tristana* with an increasingly frantic heroine, desperate to achieve her goal of 'libertad honrada'. As Emilio Miró points out, she seeks 'amor, independencia, trabajo [...] tres términos no antagónicos, sino perfectamente compatibles entre sí' (*23*, p. 515), which men take for granted. Yet society, arguably represented by these three male characters, does not approve of women enjoying such opportunities. The more Tristana pushes, the more she is alienated, the more desperate and even hysterical she becomes, until society and nature (not nature of gender, but of illness leading to physical mutilation) finally rid her of all hope and desire. This notwithstanding the notion so well expressed by Luis Cernuda that 'el deseo es pregunta cuya respuesta nadie sabe'.[41] With the loss of desire comes also the loss of Tristana's voice and self, as she returns to being a passive possession of don Lope, described by him once more as 'muñeca de mi vida'.

Jagoe observes how 'Tristana is censured by Horacio, don Lope, and the narrator for being the frantic dreamer of an impossible utopia that all three characterize as excessive, unhealthy, and unnatural' (*16*, p. 132). If the reader were expected to read *Tristana* in the same light, this would be a thesis novel, all but devoid of irony, and the narrator's final, teasing words, 'Tal vez ...', would be superfluous.

---

[40] B. Pérez Galdós, *Obras completas: Cuentos Teatro y Censo*, p. 382.
[41] Cernuda, 'No decía palabras'. Quoted by Bikandi-Mejías (*5*, p. 13).

5. The Need for Control: Don Lope and Horacio

The male protagonists in this novel, don Lope and Horacio, each seek to control Tristana and deny her the independence she seeks. Don Lope has attracted considerably more reaction from critics, whose responses to this character range from sympathy, and even admiration, to condemnation.[42] Horacio has tended to receive less critical attention on the grounds that, as a character, he is 'the least interesting' (*10*, p. 96). Nevertheless, while in Leon Livingstone's view 'his behavior falls within the category of the predatory male' (*18*, p. 97), for others, including Engler, Horacio's significance lies in 'what he comes to represent for Tristana' (*10*, p. 96).

While don Lope and Horacio seek to control Tristana in fairly typical patriarchal fashion, there is also a point where Tristana can be seen to control or create an alternative representation of Horacio, albeit within what might be described as an imaginary space of her own. Nevertheless, within the 'reality' of the novel, Tristana is largely a victim of the control of these two men as well, of course, as of the patriarchal society they can be seen to represent. The extent to which she is also a victim of nature as Livingstone maintains is, of course, debatable.

The need to overcome patriarchal power and control is clearly crucial in the quest for female emancipation and whether or not one believes *Tristana* to be essentially a pro or anti-feminist novel will depend, to some extent, on the interpretation of the roles played by these two male characters and the manner in which they exercise control.

For the famous French feminist Hélène Cixous, there is a distinct difference between the way men and women exercise control

---

[42] Livingstone appears to sympathise with don Lope (*18*) and Nimetz to admire him (see n. 39, above), while Kay Engler sees him as 'evil and monstruous' (*10,* p. 95).

or power, as she distinguishes between what she describes as 'woman's powers', being 'a *question of power over oneself*, in other words of a relation not based on mastery but on availability (disponibilité)', as opposed to 'the kind of power that is the will to supremacy [...] that power is always a power over others'.[43] This view is in some ways similar to that of Luce Irigaray, for whom power is a male obsession and who is herself anxious not to 'fall into the trap of wanting to exercise power'.[44] In Julia Kristeva's less essentialist vision of society, the fact of being born male or female would no longer determine the subject's position in relation to power and thus the very nature of power itself would be transformed.[45] Toril Moi argues along similar lines: 'Feminism is not simply about rejecting power, but about transforming the existing power structures — and, in the process, transforming the very *concept* of power itself' (p. 148).

This consideration of the nature of power and the role of biologism is clearly relevant to a full understanding of a novel such as *Tristana*, where the heroine becomes increasingly unhappy with such existing power structures and the limitations these place upon her. The kind of power Tristana appears to wish to exercise from an early point in the novel is the kind described by Cixous as 'woman's powers', i.e. predominantly over herself, as opposed to 'the will to supremacy [...] over others'.

It is clear from the outset of the novel that this latter form of power is the kind sought and exercised by don Lope, who seems constantly to need to control Tristana. His 'will to supremacy' over her is not only physical, but mental and emotional. Minter points out that his very name, Garrido, suggests *garras*, 'claws', and his propensity to hold on to Tristana. We are told how, from the beginning, 'Don Lope le cautivaba con esmero la imaginación,

---

[43] Hélène Cixous, 'Entretien avec Françoise van Rossum-Guyon', *Revue des Sciences Humaines*, 168 (Oct.–Dec. 1977), pp. 483–84. Quoted and translated by Toril Moi, *Sexual/Textual Politics: Feminist Literary Theory* (London: Routledge, 1985), p. 124.
[44] Luce Irigaray, *Ce sexe qui n'en est pas un* (Paris: Minuit, 1977), p. 161.
[45] See Toril Moi, p. 172.

sembrando en ella ideas que fomentaran la conformidad con
semejante vida; estimulaba la fácil disposición de la joven para
idealizar las cosas, para verlo todo como no es, o como nos conviene
o nos gusta que sea' (12). When she shows signs of escaping from
his clutches, he is quick to threaten her: 'Si te sorprendo en algún
mal paso, te mato, cree que te mato' (18). According to Leon
Livingstone, however, it would seem that don Lope is justified in
attempting to prevent Tristana's liberation, and the novel serves as 'a
defense of the law of Nature, which ultimately must always triumph'
(*18*, p. 93).

    But are such a situation and such reinforcement of patriarchal
power both natural and desirable? Even if, as Livingstone and others
have been anxious to stress, by the end of the novel the balance
might be seen to have been redressed between their ages as 'the
maturing of Tristana and her physical suffering have aged her to the
point that although only twenty-five she now looks forty' (*18*, p.
98)? Does that make it all right and all natural in the end? Can we
really pat don Lope on the back and call him 'a wonderful old rake'?

    Don Lope is also described by Livingstone as 'a worldly-wise
old roué' (p. *98*), which is perhaps closer to the mark — he is
certainly crafty and wily. Notwithstanding the double standard in
sexual behaviour, to have seduced a young girl entrusted into his
care — 'a los dos meses de llevársela aumentó con ella la lista ya
larguísima de sus batallas ganadas a la inocencia'(10) — thus
dishonouring her and rendering her virtually unmarriageable in the
society of the time, can hardly be described by any decent-thinking
person as wonderful behaviour. And, of course, don Lope prided
himself on having similarly dishonoured countless other victims, and
presumably destroyed many a life. Yet he is not presented in totally
negative terms, far from it, as the narrator is keen to stress, tongue
almost permanently in cheek: 'conviene hacer toda la luz posible en
torno del don Lope, para que no se le tenga por mejor ni por más
malo de lo que era realmente' (4). Certainly, Galdós appears to strike
a fine balance in the representation of don Lope in this novel, as
opposed to the harsher approach apparent in the original manuscript
and the more sympathetic portrayal of the character by Buñuel in his

film version of the work.[46] Ultimately, however, as Edward Friedman so aptly observes, 'Don Lope is served by an anachronistic and retrogressive code, and his opposition to progress is mirrored on an individual level in his seduction of Tristana, the figurative destruction of her future' (*11*, p. 207).

As Tristana 'iba cobrando aborrecimiento y repugnancia a la miserable vida que llevaba bajo el poder de don Lope Garrido' (13) and rebels against it, don Lope, realizing that the heavy-handed approach is not going to work, employs other tactics in order to keep her under his control. He admits to her: 'Te miro como hija o como esposa: segun me convenga.' (40). This, of course, adds to Tristana's confusion, as when she is trying to explain the situation to Horacio, she cannot find the right words: 'No estoy casada con mi marido ..., digo, con mi papá ..., digo, con ese hombre ...' (35). Hence Aldaraca's description of the relationship as 'the paradigmatic incestuous romance' (*1*, p. 236), on the grounds that both the age difference and the paternal authority and control exercised render the relationship incestuous.

Don Lope repeatedly twists the situation to his advantage to enable him to retain control. For Tristana's 'tirano' is not only 'worldly-wise', as Livingstone and Engler have both described him, but wily and selfish. While he may not be totally 'monstruous' as Engler sees him (there are occasions when he does show some genuine affection for Tristana as well, of course, as generosity towards friends), don Lope knows his days as a successful womanizer are drawing to a close and it would suit him very nicely to have a beautiful young woman like Tristana constantly at his beck and call. A young woman he can control. And this he is determined to do.

To ensure his control over Tristana, don Lope plays a very clever game. Having first been given control of this young girl at a vulnerable stage in her life, don Lope was in a strong position which he abused. Nevertheless, he justified this abuse, convincing himself

---

[46] A photocopy of the manuscript is conserved in the Casa-Museo Pérez Galdós, Caja 19, Núm. 1, and the original in the Biblioteca Nacional in Madrid.

'Bien me la he ganado' (11), notwithstanding his declared belief in the freedom of the individual. At the same time, he is no fool, soon recognizing and acknowledging to Tristana 'Eres una mujer superior' (32) and humouring her when it suits him by providing her with instruction and encouraging her with such platitudes as: 'No sabemos sino que tienes alas. ¿Hacia dónde volarás?' (76). But Tristana will not be allowed to fly. Nature, don Lope, Society, all will conspire to ensure there is no possibility of that. Neither will she find happiness in love as, again, don Lope is quick to realize that her relationship with Horacio is doomed — 'Incompatibilidad de caracteres ...' (103) — so he can afford to play a watching and a waiting game, cleverly twisting the situation to his advantage. Indeed, Engler speaks of his 'diabolical cleverness' as 'don Lope plays with Tristana's emotions, alternately giving her more freedom and pulling her back towards him; at times being understanding, affectionate, and paternal; at other times, becoming insanely jealous and tyrannical. Tristana is left emotionally unsure of herself, and her feelings toward don Lope become increasingly ambivalent' (*10*, p. 106).

Aitor Bikandi-Mejías describes don Lope's power over Tristana as 'un poder satánico' (*5*, p. 57) and there are many examples in the text stressing the 'misteriosa autoridad' which he exercises over her. Tristana herself describes don Lope's treatment of women as 'obra del demonio', and from the time she first becomes aware of the pain in her leg, attributes this to don Lope, writing to Horacio: 'Es que don Lope me ha pegado su reuma' and furthermore insisting that in this way 'mi tirano se ha vengado de mis desdenes' (69).

Of course, once Tristana loses her leg, don Lope knows she will remain under his control for ever: '¡Sujeta para siempre! ¡Ya no más desviaciones de mi!'. He does, nevertheless, have the grace to acknowledge: 'Triste es mi victoria, pero cierta.' He also acknowledges: 'Quiso alejarse de mí, quiso volar; pero no contaba con su destino.' She is back under his control, for don Lope is used to getting what he wants and 'cuando se me escapa lo que quiero... me lo trae atadito de pies y manos' (87).

Don Lope knows that Horacio will not want Tristana now, and also knows that she will be equally disiullusioned when they meet again and she realizes that her lover is, in any case, not the man she had created in her imagination. So he plays the situation for all it is worth, even offering to write out her letters to Horacio if she dictates them to him when she finds herself unable to write, knowing she has already reverted to her earlier doll-like state: 'Al soltar la pluma, cayó la muñeca infeliz en gran abatimiento' (86). In his role as wise father, don Lope is well aware that the best way of achieving his objective is not to stand in the way of the doomed lovers, but actively to push them together in the almost certain knowledge that they will each then recoil from the other.

This, of course, is exactly what happens. Tristana herself was fearful of their meeting, aware to some extent that she had all but re-created her lover in her imagination during his absence and would inevitably be disillusioned by the real Horacio. Nevertheless, we read: 'Sorpresa de Tristana, que en el primer momento casi le vio como a un extraño' (99). Horacio, for his part, when pushed by don Lope to declare his intentions, takes fright, protesting: 'Tristana es enemiga irreconciliable del matrimonio. ¿No lo sabía usted?', to which the wily old hypocrite insists '¿Yo?... No' (102). At the end of this meeting with his one-time rival, don Lope is extremely pleased with himself and 'muy gozoso, restregándose las manos, decía para su sayo: "incompatabilidad de caracteres ... incompatibilidad absoluta, diferencias irreductibles"' (103).

On the face of it, Tristana returns to being what don Lope describes as 'muñeca de mi vida' (82), implying she is once more under his control which, to some extent, she is. On the other hand, although don Lope's old age is spent very contentedly licking his lips and his fingers in delight at Tristana's culinary treats, he has had to cede some control in deference to that exercised by the aunts, who leave him little alternative but to go against all his proclaimed beliefs and embrace the institution of marriage, in order to secure both his own and Tristana's future financial comfort. All this is, of course, just as much to his benefit as hers, if not more so, as she is seen to remain indifferent to all worldly matters. He is, however, also seen accompanying her to church, another *volte face* which implies at least a certain relaxation of dominant control on his part. But then, by this time, perhaps don Lope's need for such absolute control is less.

Horacio can be seen to exercise control in a different way from don Lope, but although coming from a different position, he still clearly needs to control in a fundamentally patriarchal fashion. Nevertheless, this is not immediately apparent as in the case of don Lope. Indeed, when we first meet Horacio he seems to have been almost as much a victim of such control as has Tristana, having been dominated by his grandfather to the extent of actually being tied to his desk: 'como medida preventiva le ataba las piernas a las patas de la mesa-escritorio para que no saliese' (26). The irony here is considerable, but while Horacio escapes, Tristana's fear, '¿He de estar encerrada toda mi vida?' (32), is to be realized.

At first, however, Horacio does indeed promise to be Tristana's knight in shining armour, but sadly not in the terms she needed and he appeared to offer. Tristana is quick to explain her hopes and ambitions to him; indeed, his love seems to fuel her confidence that they might be realized as we are told: 'Con el amor había nuevos focos de luz en su inteligencia' (34). But ultimately the light and knowledge for which Tristana so yearns are to be denied her, even by Horacio, hence her bewildered protest: 'No me hables a mí de dulces tinieblas. Quiero luz, más luz, siempre más luz' (71).

For Horacio is not the 'new man' he at first appears. Despite his apparent sympathy for Tristana's ambitions — 'Tú resolverás quizás el problema de la mujer libre' (45) — Horacio, too, ultimately needs to be in control: 'Había soñado en Tristana la mujer subordinada al hombre en inteligencia y en voluntad.' This would, of course, deny her the free will and expression he himself had been denied as a boy by his grandfather who 'no consentía, en suma, que el chico tuviese voluntad' (27). Also like Tristana, Horacio had endured a time when 'esperaba y esperaba siempre mejores tiempos' but, unlike her, his 'fe en su destino' (26) was more assured.

When the young couple first meet, it looks as if they were made for each other, but at this stage the attraction was essentially romantic, founded on 'el ansia inextinguible de sus corazones sedientos' (30) and manifesting itself as 'todo amor, idealismo y arrullo' (25). Yet notwithstanding his profession as a painter and the bohemian existence this might suggest, Horacio is a conventional person and his views on marriage and the family, unlike Tristana's, conform quite closely to society's customs. He is really seeking a woman who will 'ser mi compañero de toda la vida; ayudarme y sostenerme con su cariño' and asks Tristana: '¿Te parece que hay un oficio mejor, ni arte más hermoso? Hacer feliz a un hombre que te hará feliz, ¿qué más?' (55). But for Tristana, of course, there is more, she wants her own 'oficio' which will make her financially independent. When she starts to prove herself talented and perhaps capable of realizing this ambition, writing to him of her progress in languages under the tutelage of doña Malvina, he takes fright, responding: 'Temo que la *seña* Malvina te contagie de su fealdad seca y hombruna. No te me vuelvas muy filósofa, no te encarames a las estrellas' (65). In this reflection of the aspirations, similarly denied, of Galdós's earlier eponymous heroine of the novel *Gloria*, we witness the traditional male threat that a clever woman risks losing her feminine attraction and consequently the love and protection of her man, in line with Nietzsche's warning: 'When a woman has scholarly inclinations, there is usually something wrong with her sexually'. [47]

In this way, of course, male power and control is retained, for as is widely acknowledged: 'Knowledge is power', hence the knowledge Tristana desires — 'Quiero saber, saber, saber' (67) — is ultimately denied. For this, Horacio must take his share of the blame, as she herself recognizes, telling him: 'Eres responsable de la tragedia que puede ocurrir ...' (66).

---

[47] Gloria was also ultimately forced to deny her own conviction: 'Tú puedes volar hasta los astros; no te arrastres por la tierra' (*OC, N1, 569*). Nietzsche's words are quoted by Christine Battersby, *Gender and Genius* (London: The Women's Press, 1989), p. 122. Similarly, Sara Delamont and Lorna Duffin quote Edmund Leach's more recent assertion (1968) that higher education for women 'is markedly hostile to sensuality', *The Nineteenth Century Woman* (London: Croom Helm, 1978), p. 17.

Neither is Horacio the soul mate Tristana believed from the beginning she had found — 'Te quise desde que nací' (23) she insisted in one of her early letters to him. Later, of course, as Diane Urey points out, her letters reveal to the reader that Tristana's ideal of love and of a lover ultimately efface his material existence for her. Urey stresses the fact that 'the epistolary form, because it appears more "written" than other types of novels, offers an especially apt means for displaying language's consciousness of its intrinsic irony'.[48] Yet through language, as observed, Tristana is able to exercise a form of control over her lover, insisting 'Déjame que te fabrique [...] que te componga', re-inventing him as she herself puts it to him: 'te invento [...] a mi gusto, según mis ideas' (78).

For although Horacio had appeared sympathetic to her ideas he had initially to some extent, like don Lope, been playing a waiting game: waiting for the moment when Tristana would give in and surrender to his control. When Tristana attempts to make it clear to him 'que sirvo, que podré servir para las cosas grandes; pero que decididamente no sirvo para las pequeñas', we are told: 'Lo que Horacio le contestó perdióse en la oleada de ternezas que vino después' (56). Thus it seems that Horacio is doing little more than humouring Tristana in her talk of initiative and independence, in the belief that his loving charm will soon convince her of the error of her ways. Despite her insistence: 'Nada de matrimonio, para no andar a la greña por aquello de quién tiene las faldas y quién no' (49), Horacio nevertheless 'se complacía en suponer que el tiempo iría templando en ella la fiebre de ideación [...] haciéndola más mujer, más doméstica, más corriente y útil' (48).

Horacio's waiting game, however, unlike don Lope's, does not pay off although, ironically, Tristana does ultimately become 'más doméstica, más corriente y útil' married to don Lope and, on the face of it, still subject to his control, even though he himself had impressed upon her: 'Tú no puedes ni debes ser de nadie, sino de ti misma' (76).

---

[48] Diane Urey, *Galdós and the Irony of Language* (Cambridge: Cambridge University Press, 1982), p. 86.

Nevertheless, one might argue that in Tristana's virtual rejection of 'todo lo terrestre' on which we are told she looks 'con sumo desdén' (110), the withdrawal of her voice from the text effectively parallelling her withdrawal from reality, she is at least in part exercising the 'woman's powers' described by Cixous as being over oneself, thereby limiting the amount of patriarchal power and control exercised by don Lope over her.

6. The Search for Identity: Tristana

'Aquí estoy' declares Tristana, as she shakes off 'la estopa de la muñeca', demanding '¿No ves cómo pienso cosas grandes?' (13). Thus soon after her introduction by the narrator, we are confronted with the heroine's insistence not only that we acknowledge her existence as an autonomous being, but also that we recognize her substance, which should be apparent to us: '¿No ves?'.

So here she is and we are told of her 'conciencia de no ser una persona vulgar' (13). But what is she and who is she? What are 'las cosas grandes' of which she is thinking and to which she is to refer so many times? What is her identity and what is her destiny? Who or what is responsible for the answers to these questions? Can they be answered? 'Tal vez' appears to be the narrator's slippery answer at the end of this ambiguous novel.

Central to the many ambiguities of this work lies that of the identity of its eponymous heroine. The whole concept of identity remains a complex one which continues to intrigue and confuse contemporary writers in general and feminist writers in particular. Much work has been done on identity theory on the literary, social, and psychological level and, of course, in Lacan's elaboration of Freudian theory, rather than a unitary, coherent self, identity is perceived as plural, indeterminate, even illusory. Hélène Cixous insists 'I never ask myself "who am I?" (qui suis-je?), I ask myself "who are I?" (qui sont-je?) — an untranslatable phrase. Who can say who I are, how many I are … ?'[49] The point is stressed in Rosa Montero's latest novel, *La hija del caníbal* (1997), where the heroine Lucía concludes: 'La identidad es una cosa confusa y extraordinaria'.[50]

---

[49] Hélène Cixous, Preface to *The Hélène Cixous Reader*, ed. S. Sellers (London: Routledge, 1994), p. xvii.

[50] Rosa Montero, *La hija del caníbal* (Madrid: Espasa Narrativa), p. 335.

All this is evident in the case of Tristana, notwithstanding our awareness of her as an artistic construct and ultimately, as Akiko Tsuchiya stresses, 'a sign on the page' (*35*, p. 57). Various identities are attached to our heroine from the beginning, as she is described variously by the narrator, the neighbours, her guardian and seducer, don Lope, and her lover, Horacio, as 'una muñeca', 'una petaca', 'de papel plástico', 'una dama japonesa', and then ultimately as 'una mujer superior'.

Her relationship to don Lope is equally ambiguous: she is seen as 'hija', 'sobrina', 'esposa', 'cautiva', and 'esclava'. This shifting identity and the constant reference to her possessing wings have recently led Gordon Minter to liken Tristana to a butterfly, in an insightful study which could also be linked to Galdós's earlier novel, *Gloria*, where the analogy is closer as the heroine shuts herself away and 'como el laborioso insecto, ha tejido un capullo y, quedándose dentro, con intención, sin duda, de no salir sino con alas, o sea en espíritu' (*OC, NI*, 606).[51] In Noël Valis's view, Tristana's constant 'metamorphoses' exemplify Galdós's 'conception of human personality which is at once open-ended and disquieting, supremely modern and ultimately elusive' (*37*, p. 208).

As we have seen, Tristana herself envisages new potential professional identities — identities as yet uncoined and unrecognized in Spain. For 'las cosas grandes' to which she aspires, the choices necessary for her to forge the identity she desires, are denied her because of her gender. As her maid and confidante Saturna is quick to point out: 'Para eso hay que ser hombre, señorita', adding 'La maldita enagua estorba para eso, como para montar a caballo'(15). Society's restrictions, symbolized here by 'la maldita enagua' and elsewhere in Galdós's works by 'el maldito corsé', deny

---

[51] Gordon Minter, 'Butterflies, Dolls, and Gender Roles: Japanese Things in *Tristana*', in Lisa Condé & Gordon Minter, *Tristana,* Occasional Papers, 22 (Bristol: Department of Hispanic, Portuguese and Latin American Studies, University of Bristol, 1997), pp. 16–31.

women such full freedom of choice as enjoyed by men.[52] Hence the novel as a *Bildungsroman* is frustrated.

Judith Gardiner points out that while the traditional *Bildungsroman* chronicles a young man's identity crisis in a known social world, the female novel of development has its own concerns — apprenticeship to social constraint or sudden awakening — that do not fit a linear male model of steady progress.[53]

From what might be seen as Tristana's 'sudden awakening' as 'se cambiaba en sangre y médula de mujer la estopa de la muñeca' (13), she increasingly rebels against the attempts of others to create an identity for her. Don Lope had sought to control Tristana's thoughts and actions completely, 'imponiéndole su voluntad con firmeza endulzada, a veces con mimos o carantoñas, y destruyendo en ella toda iniciativa que no fuera de cosas accesorias y sin importancia' (3).

This is arguably a feminist issue of which Galdós had been aware for some time, notwithstanding his own occasional ambivalence in the matter. As early as 1871, in 'La mujer del filósofo', he had stressed female vulnerability to such control of her being, explaining:

> El alma de la mujer, que es más flexible y movediza que
> su compañero en goces y desdichas, cede prontamente a
> la influencia exterior, adopta las ideas y los sentimientos
> que se le imponen, y concluye por no ser sino lo que el
> hombre quiere que sea. (*OC, NIII*, 1425)

As Pedro Monlau was to reiterate: 'El hombre hace a la mujer'.[54] This notion of woman as a malleable being, conceding man's desire

---

[52] Notably in *Realidad*, where Augusta rebels against 'este compás social, de esta educación puritana y meticulosa, que nos desfigura el alma como el maldito corsé nos desfigura el cuerpo' (*OC*, CTC, 127).

[53] Judith Gardiner, 'Mind Mother: Psychoanalysis and Feminism', in *Making a Difference: Feminist Literary Criticism*, ed. Gayle Greene and Coppelia Kahn (London: Methuen, 1985), p. 126.

[54] Pedro Monlau, *Higiene del matrimonio o el libro de los casados* (Paris: Garnier, 1892), p. 129.

to form or reform her to his liking, is explored in a number of Galdós's novels and often reinforced with the image of the *muñeca* which Tristana, of course, is anxious to discard. She is determined not to be formed by a male-dominated society or to conform to the image of the empty-headed doll she appears at the very beginning of the novel. As Tsuchiya explains: 'Tristana begins as a blank slate upon which first the narrator and later she herself will forge an artistic identity' (*35*, p. 334).

The narrator first sketches his heroine 'de papel' before telling us that she answers to the name of Tristana. Contrasting with the many overtones of 'tristeza' in our heroine's first name, however, we are then given Tristana's surname of Reluz, with its symbolic overtones of a vision or insight beyond the ordinary. Later, and perhaps significantly, Tristana expresses her determination that any child she might bear would retain her name and identity, explaining to her lover Horacio: 'La Naturaleza me da más derechos que a ti … Y se llamará como yo, con mi apellido nada más' (50).

As Tristana assumes a voice in the text, so she claims an identity of her own. Her voice becomes increasingly dominant as her letters take over the central part of the novel and, as Hazel Gold has pointed out, 'es evidente que el ejercicio de la palabra por Tristana, es decir, de su prerrogativa autorial, entra en juego casi desde el comienzo de la novela y le ofrece la mejor oportunidad para forjarse una identidad concreta' (*12*, p. 664). This is true, despite the point stressed by Silvia Tubert that 'no hay identidad *pura* o *autónoma* en términos absolutos' since it is not possible to 'constituirse como sujeto sin pasar por un proceso de identificación con los otros', hence an individual identity is inevitably one of 'autonomía relativa' (*36*, p. 238).

We are told how, from the beginning, 'don Lope le cautivaba con esmero la imaginación' and it is ultimately only within her imagination that our heroine can totally escape from her destiny as *muñeca*. Within the 'reality' of the novel, she does manage to show talent and potential, but is unable to pursue these to the point of attaining the 'libertad honrada' she so desires, the professions to which she aspires being inaccessible to her. As Gold observes, 'escribir cartas, al contrario, representa una ocupación aceptable, hasta elogiable, para las mujeres de la España decimonónica' (*12*, p. 664.). One might argue in the terms of Cixous that 'only in language was there possibility of disruption and revolution'.[55]

Tristana recognizes that the main obstacle to her realizing her potential identity within the society of her time is her gender. This fact, and her lover's failure to acknowledge it, frustrates her to the point where, citing Lady Macbeth who, she explains, 'me ha sido siempre simpática', she adds: 'no entenderás lo que aquello quiere decir, ni yo te lo explico, porque sería como echar margaritas a ...' (67).

And indeed, for all his bohemian appearance as some kind of 'new man', Horacio does not understand. Furthermore, he is anxious that Tristana should retain her 'natural' feminine qualities of passivity and inferiority. Happy at the beginning to take on the role of teacher to Tristana, when her talent as a painter threatens to match or even surpass his own he is quick to withdraw, just as she is quick to recognize the potential damage to his male ego and reassure him: 'Tú eres el rey de los pintores', insisting she will be content to 'seguir tus huellas, siempre a distancia, se entiende ...' (44).

For Horacio, while initially expressing sympathy and admiration for Tristana's ideas and rationally accepting many of them, ultimately sought 'la esposa que vive de la savia moral e intelectual del esposo y que con los ojos y con el corazón de él ve y siente' (45). But Tristana wants to see and feel for herself, and her frustration is manifest: 'Es que vivimos sin movimiento, atadas con mil ligaduras ...' (15). But her quest for knowledge is met with the response: 'No te hagas tan sabia. Me asustas.' She herself is aware of the negative effect Horacio's reaction could have on her, as she acknowledges, 'con todo mi *marisabidillismo* (ve apuntando las palabras que invento), yo me mato si tú me abandonas' (66).

Here Tristana, just like the eponymous heroine of Galdós' earlier novel, *Gloria*, is seen to reach for the stars in her search for an autonomous and meaningful identity of her own. In each case, the

---

[55] See Janet Todd, *Feminist Literary History* (Cambridge: Polity Press, 1988), p. 56.

image of wings is repeatedly used to denote these characters' potential for individual reasoning and action, but the society in which they live is determined that 'las alas' must be definitively 'cortadas'. Although written some sixteen years earlier, the heroine's quest in *Gloria* is, in essence, the same as Tristana's, as she assures herself: 'Tú puedes volar hasta los astros ...' (*OC, NI*, 569).

Just as Tristana is discouraged from reaching for the stars or 'las cosas grandes' which occupy her mind, so Gloria is warned to conform: 'Mi padre me ha dicho varias veces que si no corto las alas al pensamiento, voy a ser muy desgraciada. Vengan, pues, las tijeras ...'. Yet soon we are told she allows her wings to grow again, as her inner voice insists: 'Rebélate, rebélate. Tu inteligencia es superior' (*OC, NI*, 579).

Similarly, while Horacio wants a wife to 'ayudarme y sostenerme con su cariño' and therefore hopes that in time Tristana will become 'más doméstica, más corriente y útil' (48), her desire for an autonomous identity increases, as she reasons:

Eso de que dos que se aman han de volverse iguales y han de pensar lo mismo, no me cabe a mi en la cabeza. ¿A qué esa confusión de caracteres? Sea cada cual como Dios le ha hecho, y siendo distintos, se amarán más. (66)

These and many more of the ideas expressed by the heroine in this novel are clearly of a feminist nature, although no direct mention is made of any contemporary feminist movement or writings, and Tristana appears largely confined within her own predicament and domestic sphere. Nevertheless, her insistence 'que sirvo, que podría servir para las cosas grandes, pero decididamente no sirvo para las pequeñas' clearly reflects the contemporary feminist Concepción Arenal's contention that 'la actividad de la mujer, imposibilitada de emplearse en cosas grandes, se emplea en las pequeñas' (*4*, p. 64).

Here again Tristana can be seen to reject the traditional expectations of her gender as she insists: 'Me parezco a los hombres en que ignoro lo que cuesta una arroba de patatas' (48). Like men, of course, she does not want to know of such matters because her sights are set on 'las cosas grandes' traditionally reserved for them. The careers she first dreams of are not available to her, as Saturna quickly makes clear, impressing upon her from the beginning that 'sólo tres carreras pueden seguir las que visten faldas: o casarse, que carrera es, o el teatro ..., vamos, ser cómica, que es buen modo de vivir, o ... no quiero nombrar lo otro. Figúraselo' (14). Tristana is, of course, as opposed to marriage as is don Lope, albeit with a very different rationale, as she explains to Horacio: 'Aspiro a no depender de nadie, ni del hombre que adoro [...] No sabré amar por obligación; sólo en la libertad comprendo mi fé constante y mi adhesión sin límites' (61). Acting, however, does appear to be one of the few professions open to her which might allow her to achieve the independence she craves, but she is unsure of her talent in this area. She does prove to have talent in those areas she is able to try, such as painting and languages, although there is little advice or information available to suggest how she might gainfully utilize such talent. Although many critics stress the fact that Tristana does not seem to know what she wants, she is clear on her essential goal: 'Libertad honrada es mi tema' (49). Yet as Saturna was also quick to point out from the start: 'Libertad ... esta palabra no suena bien en boca de mujeres' (14).

Other critics suggest that Tristana's instability and vivid imagination have been inherited from her mother, doña Josefina, who rejected the reality of the present for the romanticism of historical literature. However, while her mother looked to the past, Tristana's sights are set very much on the future, as she herself makes clear: 'Yo quiero vivir, ver mundo y enterarme de por qué y para qué nos han traído a esta tierra en que estamos. Yo quiero vivir y ser libre' (14).

Although literary allusions and games abound in her letters to Horacio, the identities Tristana assumes are not always of a romantic nature, as we have seen, in her wish to establish a more independent identity. Earlier she had expressed her horror and dismay when reflecting on the insubstantial education afforded her by her mother:

> Mi pobre mamá no pensó más que en darme la
> educación insustancial de las niñas que aprenden para
> llevar un buen yerno a casa, a saber: un poco de piano, el
> indispensable barniz de francés y qué sé yo ... tonterías.
> (44)

Interestingly, in the original manuscript, Galdós did at first attribute some of Tristana's shortcomings to 'las ideas imbuidas por su madre', but then changed this to 'su descuidada educación'.[56]

Much of the frustration expressed by Tristana in her letters to Horacio exactly parallels that expressed in letters to Galdós by Concha-Ruth Morell, and her presence as an aspect of the heroine's identity clearly cannot be ignored. Both crave the autonomous identity they appear to have been denied and find themselves ultimately frustrated by fate, circumstances, nature ... or is it society? Where the greater emphasis is seen to lie will depend on individual perspective, for no definitive answers are offered to any of the questions posed. Like Tristana, Concha-Ruth aspired to the one decent profession she felt was open to her: acting, although it was not one to which she felt particularly suited and, indeed, she did not prove particularly successful. Her lack of success was compounded by her illness, while in Tristana's case her illness precludes her from even trying. Nevertheless, Tristana does not give up her quest for an autonomous identity until the amputation of her leg, seen by Bridget Aldaraca not only as a kind of psychological castration, but as 'a destruction or fragmentation of the will' (*1*, p. 244), at which point we are told by the narrator that Tristana 'no parecía la misma'. When don Lope asks her '¿Y esta inspiración y esos arranques?', she simply replies: 'No me ocurre nada' (90).

The subsequent withdrawal of Tristana's voice from the text is parallelled with her reversion to being don Lope's 'muñeca'. Significantly, this movement is crystallized in the moment when Tristana drops her pen, unable to finish the letter in which she has just told Horacio of her impending operation: 'Al soltar la pluma,

---

[56] See Michael Allen Schnepf, 'Galdós's *Tristana* Manuscript: Don Lope Garrido', *Romance Notes*, 31 (1990–91), 11–17.

cayó la muñeca infeliz en grande abatimiento' (86). As she reverts to being, in Gilbert and Gubar's terms, 'a creation "penned" by man', Tristana's 'ingenio superior sufría un eclipse total'.[57] Nevertheless, we are told, 'tanta pasividad y mansedumbre [...] agradaron a don Lope' (90).

Critics continue to disagree over Tristana's final mental state. Catherine Jagoe sees her resignation as suggesting 'a sort of internal death' (*17*, 138) while, at the other extreme, for Gordon Minter 'she has achieved emotional, psychological and spiritual independence, so that her mission is accomplished rather than aborted' (*22*, p. xxiv).

The end itself, where Tristana marries her ancient seducer, don Lope, I see as tragic and a gross parody of marriage. According to the narrator, Tristana 'lo aceptó con indiferencia; había llegado a mirar todo lo terrestre con sumo desdén ... Casi no se dio cuenta de que la casaron [...] encasillándola en un hueco honroso de la sociedad' (110). I cannot believe this is meant to be a description of a happily married woman, as some critics conclude Tristana to be. It is don Lope who licks his fingers in delight at his wife's new culinary skills, not Tristana. Neither can I accept Jagoe's recent contention that Galdós is appropriating feminist terms for anti-feminist ends (*16*, p. 182), or Livingstone's view that the novel serves to illustrate a natural rather than a socially acceptable conclusion (*18*). For as Galdós himself was to stress in 1893, the year following the publication of *Tristana*: 'Vivimos como antes, rodeados de injusticias, de desigualdades'.[58]

However, in answer to the heroine's earlier frustrated question: '¿No ves?', it is clear that the 'eye' of each individual beholder as well as the 'I' or 'yo' of our heroine may well see and perceive differently. At the same time, aspects of perception and self-perception, depiction and self-depiction, deception and self-

---

[57] And, indeed, 'penned in' by him. See Sandra M. Gilbert and Susan Gubar, *The Madwoman in the Attic: The Woman Writer and the Nineteenth-Century Literary Imagination* (New Haven: Yale University Press, 1984), p. 13.

[58] *Obras inéditas,* II, ed. Alberto Ghiraldo (Madrid: Renacimiento, 1923), p.244.

deception, constantly fluctuate, as author, narrator, character, and reader all mediate and re-create.

For Tsuchiya, Tristana's defence of feminist principles is inseparable from her creative role as, rather than conforming to the role of the woman as a text to be written, she goes further to impose her own text on the male subject in her attempts to create or re-create Horacio (*35*, p. 339). Yet ultimately, and ironically, perhaps it is Horacio who comes closest to recognizing the essential nature of Tristana's identity, as he suggests:

> Quizá ve más que todos nosotros; quizá su mirada perspicua, o cierto instinto de adivinación concedido a las mujeres superiores, ve la sociedad futura que nosotros no vemos. (102)

This would be in line with Galdós's own assertion in 1917 that 'el día en que la mujer consiga emanciparse, el mundo será distinto' and Pardo Bazán's insistence in 1896 that 'el número de mujeres verdaderamente superiores, sin que por esto sean célebres, sería incalculable', to be followed by her lament in 1901: '¡Vivimos, particularmente en esto, tan atrasados! ¡Sería tan dificultoso romper nuestra costra de incultura, modificar nuestro criterio, propiamente musulmán, en cuanto se refiere a la mujer!'.[59]

Both don Lope and Horacio had recognized Tristana's potential, the former declaring 'No sabemos más sino que tienes alas' (76) and Horacio describing her as possessing 'unas alas de extraordinaria fuerza para subirse a los espacios sin fin' (103). But these wide open spaces are not open to Tristana who, with wings clipped, is firmly enclosed within 'un hueco honroso de la sociedad' (110). 'Honrada' but not 'libre'. The identity she sought and to which she felt she was entitled was denied her, as she is left with what Emilio Miró so succinctly describes as 'la imposibilidad de

---

[59] Galdós, reported by Ángel Martín (his coachman in 1917) in *Excelsior* (Mexico City), 11 Nov. 1917. Pardo Bazán, *La vida contemporánea* (1896–1915), ed. Carmen Bravo-Villasante (Madrid: Editorial Magisterio Español, 1972), p. 118.

ser', for ultimately, 'las alas cortadas o la pierna cortada, todo es lo mismo' (*23*, p. 520).

In contrast to the overt irony apparent in the name of the eponymous protagonist of Galdós's early novel, *Doña Perfecta*, the name Tristana Reluz is clearly an appropriate one. Tristana's destiny is to be a sad one, despite her desperate quest for light — 'Quiero luz, más luz, siempre más luz' she had insisted repeatedly. Light which, as Teresa Vilarós stresses, 'aún doble, sólo brilla temporalmente para hacernos conscientes de la triste oscuridad'.[60] Tristana had implored Horacio, 'No me hables a mí de dulces tinieblas' (71), but is ultimately condemned to darkness, her light all but extinguished.

Unlike her mother, doña Josefina, who looked to a romanticized past to find her identity, Tristana looks to a potentially viable future and sees an identity which, albeit not clearly defined, is rooted in the 'libertad honrada' which nineteenth-century Spanish society denies her. As the twentieth-century American feminist, Betty Friedan, was to declare: 'Women, as well as men, can only find their identity in work that uses their full capacities'.[61] Erik Erikson defined man's identity crisis as 'the decision as to what one is and is going to be', but Friedan points out that, well into the twentieth century, women were still 'not expected to choose their human identity' due to 'a stunting or evasion of growth that is perpetuated by the feminine mystique'.[62]

Prevented from pursuing 'las cosas grandes' and assuming the identity she believes to be hers, Tristana is forced to go against her own true nature as we are told 'denegaba su propio ser' (90). She had repeatedly insisted 'que sirvo, que podría servir para las cosas

---

[60] Teresa M. Vilarós, 'Mutilación, realidad y escritura: la invención de *Tristana*', in a conference paper subsequently adapted as 'Invención simulacro y violencia en *Tristana*', in *A Sesquicentennial Tribute to Galdós 1843–1993*, ed. Linda M. Willem (Newark: Juan de la Cuesta, 1993), 121–37. Original quotation modified in published version, p. 127.

[61] Betty Friedan, *The Feminine Mystique* (London: Penguin, 1992), p. 292 (first published 1963).

[62] Erik H. Erikson, *Young Man Luther: A Study in Psychoanalysis and History* (New York: W.W. Norton, 1958), p. 15. Friedan, p. 68.

grandes, pero que decididamente no sirvo para las pequeñas'. Equally definitively, she had declared: 'No valgo, no, para encerronas de toda la vida' (14). But now she is well and truly grounded, as she focuses her energies on baking *pasteles,* to don Lope's consummate delight.

Literally reduced to playing the role of 'mujer honrada, pierna quebrada y en casa' within the social reality of the novel, Tristana withdraws from it, as her voice is withdrawn from the text. At the same time, that inner core of identity which she retains looks on 'con sumo desdén'.

7. The Buñuel Alternative

Luis Buñuel's imagination was clearly fired by the plight of Galdós's Tristana, whom he re-created for the large screen in 1970. Although the result was a work which dealt less directly with feminist issues, it is one which might be viewed as more satisfying by some feminist spectators. This is largely due to the fact that Buñuel changes the ending of *Tristana* dramatically.

Of course, it is not only the ending of the work which is changed by Buñuel. The whole setting is changed from the outskirts of Madrid to Toledo and the time brought forward from the late nineteenth century to the early 1930s, although arguably such changes have less effect on a work such as *Tristana*, described by Minter as predominantly an 'internal' novel (*22*, p. vii), than they would have had on a work such as *Fortunata y Jacinta*, so entwined in the historical and political events of the day. Nevertheless, in Andrés Amorós Guardiola's view, 'el director aragonés nos está diciendo claramente que la historia de *Tristana*, tal como él lo ve, no es una historia del siglo pasado, sino algo mucho más próximo, que brota de la España tradicional y está en las raíces mismas del presente'.[63] Similarly, Beth Miller points out how 'Tristana's dream of freedom was as doomed as Lope's of liberalization; these were impossible individually because they were impossible in Spain after the demise of the Second Republic' (*21*, p. 348).

It appears Buñuel had been interested in working on Galdós's *Tristana* for some time, but plans to film in Madrid in 1963 were refused by the authorities and it was not until late 1969 that filming was allowed to commence in Toledo, a favourite city of his youth (and a city also favoured by Galdós, after Madrid). The fact that

---

[63] Andrés Amorós Guardiola, '*Tristana*, de Galdós a Buñuel', in *Actas del primer Congreso Internacional de Estudios Galdosianos* (Las Palmas: Cabildo Insular de Gran Canaria, 1977), pp. 319–29, at p. 322

Buñuel persisted with this project, continuing to revise and recast his original script during the 60s before collaborating with Julio Alejandro on a final version, is testimony to his affinity with the work. Colin Partridge speculates that this may have had something to do with the fact that his own mother was only eighteen years old when she married the forty-two-year-old Leonardo Buñuel, as well as the film-maker's personal empathy with the figure of don Lope, which arguably contributed to the shift in approach to the portrayal of this character (*25*, p. 213).

Although much of *Tristana* is changed, much is also retained in Buñuel's film version. Other aspects are expanded: the film is less confined in terms of space than the original work, largely limited to enclosed settings; and Buñuel, as one might expect, focusses on religious symbols which do not appear in the novel, stressing the influence of the Church and particularly of the Virgin Mary.

Apart from the resolution of the work, a further major change made by Buñuel to the plot was to have Tristana actually leave don Lope to go away and live with Horacio. This means, of course, that we are not privy in the film to all the letters our heroine writes to her lover during their enforced separation, which reveal so much of her psychology. Indeed, Beth Miller observes that 'Although Tristana is perhaps the greatest of Buñuel's female creations, she seems, paradoxically, to be the one least understood by critics' (*21*, p. 340). For notwithstanding the fact observed in Chapter 1 of this Guide that the possibilities for ambiguity are greater in the novel than the film, both Galdós and Buñuel are masters of irony and the psychology of the protagonist leads to problems of interpretation in each case.

The spectator who knows Galdós's *Tristana* will almost certainly alternate between closely recognizing and at times recoiling from the various images of her offered by Buñuel, described by Miller as 'familiar stock images' which the film-maker probes. These move successively from innocent angel, obedient daughter, malleable pupil, and kept woman, on to those of rebel and, in the final anaylsis, 'archetypal bitch' (*21,* p. 353). It is, of course, this final twist to our heroine's personality by Buñuel which provokes the greatest reaction.

Buñuel's depiction of don Lope, on the other hand, generates a more sympathetic response. Engagingly played by Fernando Rey, the tyrant turned victim is pathetic and more than likely to arouse the spectator's pity, regardless of the character's previous behaviour. This shift is interesting, particularly when one looks at Galdós's original manuscript of *Tristana*, in which don Lope is actually portrayed in a harsher light than in the final published version of the novel, where the novelist strikes a finer balance. It is also interesting here to compare Miller's observation: 'Buñuel is sympathetic to Lope, with whom he sometimes identifies' (*21,* p. 356) with Lambert's corresponding comment in relation to Galdós: 'It would be consistent with the savage mood of the novel if the portraits of don Lope and Horacio were in some respects vicious self-portraits' (*17,* p. 43).[64]

For despite the many similarities between the two versions of *Tristana*, it is, as Miller stresses, 'Buñuel's consciousness that shapes the film', within which Tristana is 'essentially his creation' (*21,* p. 356) as, one might add, are both don Lope and Horacio, whose portrayal in the film has attracted less critical reaction but is arguably less sympathetic than in the novel. Apart from the fact that we are not privy to any of the details given in the novel of this character's own earlier victimization at the hands of his grand-father, Buñuel's Horacio appears harsher, as in the episode where he knocks don Lope to the ground when challenged by him to a formal duel. Colin Partridge points out that 'this cruelly humorous scene shows how distant he [don Lope] is from contemporary values; Horacio responds to his archaic attitude with a punch to don Lope's jaw like a twentieth-century American film hero' (*25,* p. 222). The significance of Horacio's role in the film is also shifted, as is that of Saturno, as Buñuel plays with one of his favourite themes: desire.

The theme of desire is, of course, also crucial in the novel, but the emphasis in the film is more overtly on the sexual and the surreal, as one might expect in Buñuel, and also more closely linked to death. Desire itself, as is widely acknowledged, can never be

---

[64] According to Fernando Rey, the fictional don Lope approaching sixty closely resembled the indomitable Luis Buñuel approaching seventy.

totally fulfilled, and through Tristana's letters in the novel Horacio can be seen to represent her impossible desire for the ideal. Hence ultimately, as Bikandi-Mejías observes, 'Tristana no necesita a Horacio a su lado, por carta es suficiente' for 'en el fondo sólo lo necesita como representante del deseo inalcanzable' (5, p. 150). In the novel, Tristana's desire is focussed on love, freedom, and knowledge, most vividly expressed in her words: 'Quiero luz, más luz, siempre más luz' and echoed in her insistence, 'Quiero saber, saber, saber ...'. Bikandi-Mejías points out that 'la búsqueda del saber, del conocimiento, ya era vista por Platón como manifestación del deseo: el amor entre personas y la búsqueda del filósofo de la verdad parten de la misma raíz'. Furthermore, of course, 'el filósofo nunca colmará su deseo de conocimiento' (5, p. 54).

Buñuel focusses less directly on feminist issues, although he retains one or two key ideas; for example in the film Tristana talks to Horacio about her desire to work, maybe teaching the piano, insisting 'que sirvo para las cosas grandes', but Horacio does not reply; instead he quietens her with kisses. Similarly, don Lope is shown to want to keep women in their place, despite his liberal talk of freedom. When Saturna suggests taking Tristana out for some fresh air, he actually quotes the proverb so applicable to but never mentioned in the novel: 'La mujer honrada, pierna quebrada y en casa', and later commands the maid: 'Tú a tus cacerolas...' which is, of course, where Tristana ends up in the novel version.

As indicated, desire in the film is given greater erotic expression, although in the view of a number of critics this is latent in the novel and drawn out and developed by Buñuel. The links between sexual desire and death, eroticism and self-destruction, are more apparent in the film: Tristana's recurrent dream of don Lope's head on the phallic form of the bell clapper, for example, and the scene where she inclines over the figure of Cardinal Tavera in the sepulchre as if to kiss it. Other images of and links with death are apparent in both novel and film, including the very relationship between such a young girl and an ageing man, the frequent description/representation of Tristana's ghostly, paper-like pallor. Tristana herself, looking in the mirror, observes: 'Parezco la muerte' (92) and, also in the novel, the description of the amputated leg 'envuelto en una sábana' subsequently referred to as lying 'en el seno de aquel sepulcro que a manzanas olía', as Tristana faces 'su nueva vida, después de aquel simulacro de muerte' (89).

It is this 'new life' of Tristana's, following her declaration in both novel and film: 'Soy otra', which is so differently presented. From the many reactions to these alternatives, I should like here to quote two: one from Galdós's contemporary, Emilia Pardo Bazán, published the same year as the novel, and the other expressed by Colin Partridge in 1995, some twenty-five years after the release of Buñuel's film. According to Pardo Bazán, Galdós in his novel 'nos dejó ver un horizonte nuevo y amplio, y después corrió la cortina' (*24*, p. 141), while for Partridge, in Buñuel's version 'Tristana's triumph becomes the film's ultimate contradiction' (*25*, p. 219). Pardo Bazán's reaction will be discussed in the Conclusion, but Partridge's will be borne in mind while considering 'the Buñuel alternative' to the resolution of *Tristana*.

Both novel and film are, of course, full of contradictions and ambiguities, but the major, dramatic turn of events pursued to its ultimate conclusion by Buñuel is the total shift of power and control, in every sense and literally to the death, from don Lope to Tristana. The victimizer becomes the victim, and the victim the victimizer. Tristana's yearning in the novel for the strength of Lady Macbeth can be seen to be fully realized in the film as she adopts the 'masculine', merciless stance of her former oppressor. Yet ironically, it is precisely in this way that she differs from Galdós's Tristana, who wants to be free of the ties that bind ('Es que vivimos sin movimiento, atadas con mil ligaduras') but ultimately seeks control over her own destiny and identity, as discussed in Chapter 5, above. Buñuel's Tristana, however, seeks to exercise the other kind of power described by Cixous as 'the kind of power that is the will to supremacy [...] that power is always a power over others' (see n. 43, above).

Miller concludes that Buñuel's Tristana 'has successfully broken out of the traditional cultural conceptions of proper sex role behavior only to become more domineering, strong-minded, egoistic, spiteful, hostile, manipulative, and tough than Lope had been in his prime'. This, of course, is not the form of 'libertad' sought by Galdós's Tristana or by the majority of feminists, but rather a form of revenge exercised through the the misuse of power or, put another way, the use of the 'wrong kind' of power. Miller suggests this is the behaviour of the 'archetypal bitch', but goes on to say that 'as "bitch", Tristana has become androgynous, incorporating qualities traditionally defined as masculine as well as those considered feminine' (*21*, p. 353). This seems to imply that Buñuel's Tristana has adopted the less attractive qualities of both sexes, while arguably Galdós's Tristana aspires to the opposite, in line with Lou-Charnon Deutsch's description of women created by Galdós who 'occasionally show signs of a sexual ambiguity that could be classified as an androgynous vision anticipatory of twentieth-century prose'.[65] For Partridge, on the other hand, Buñuel's Tristana becomes 'an incarnation of female power holding together impossible contradictions born of psychological bitterness rather than physical disability' (*25*, p. 223).

It is clear that the Tristana of Buñuel's film actively seeks revenge on her former oppressor, don Lope and, in the realm of revenge, gender roles can become increasingly blurred. Otto Rank declared to Anais Nin: 'Revenge is necessary [...] to reestablish equilibrium in the emotional life' and this seems to be the case for Buñuel's Tristana, while Galdós's heroine 'lo aceptó todo con indiferencia'.[66] Does this mean, as Miller says, that the former 'is certainly a far stronger woman than the Tristana of the Galdós novel' (*21*, p. 357)? Or is it the case that the latter is strong enough to rise above 'todo lo terrestre', upon which she looks 'con sumo desdén'? Does effectively stooping to don Lope's level make Tristana essentially a stronger person, or just a harder, more dangerous one? One who is more of a 'bitch', or more of a 'man'?

---

[65] Charnon-Deutsch, *Gender and Representation: Women in Spanish Realist Fiction* (Amsterdam: John Benjamins, 1990), p. 123.
[66] Anais Nin, *The Diary of Anais Nin: 1931–1934*, ed. G. Stuhlmann (New York: Harcourt, Brace & World, 1966), p. 307.

Galdós's Tristana wanted the opportunities and advantages of a man, but she did not seek the power over others that men have traditionally exercised. Her struggle was arguably on a deeper level than that of her counterpart, hence the two heroines' separate declarations: 'Soy otra' refer not only to their distinctive metamorphoses within the respective works, but the essentially distinctive characters given to them by their respective (male) creators.

Buñuel's ending to *Tristana* is a powerful and melodramatic one, while Galdós's is left in the air with the enigmatic words, 'Tal vez', providing the only answer to the reader's questions. He clearly wanted this novel to have an open ending, originally closing with the words '¿Quién lo sabe?' which he then modified in the manuscript to 'Tal vez'. Rather than the dubious tragedy of a death, the novel has been seen as 'a warped comedy', and one that clearly lacks poetic justice. But maybe this is just the point Galdós wishes to make as an indictment of society: a society which, one way or another, will close the window of opportunity for women rather than the author who, as Pardo Bazán complained, 'corrió la cortina'.

According to some critics, Buñuel 'lleva a sus últimas consecuencias algo que ya estaba en la novela', as the film-maker is seen as resolving Galdós's open and ambiguous ending.[67] Yet even this view invites the question, is Buñuel's Tristana happier following the death of don Lope? Has the exercising of power and revenge in this way 'reestablished equilibrium in the emotional life' as predicted by Otto Rank? Bikandi-Mejías points out that, while the film's ending is also open to various interpretations, the film-script actually states: 'En su lecho, Tristana no puede descansar, víctima de una pesadilla. Por su imaginación pasan vertiginosamente las imágenes que la torturan desde hace años.' As the critic observes, 'para el guión, es obvio: pesadilla, imaginación, en la cabeza de Tristana. Para los espectadores, y para los críticos, nada está tan claro' (*5*, p. 176).

---

[67] See Cristina Martinez-Carazo, '*Tristana*: el discurso verbal frente al discurso visual', *Hispania*, 76 (1993), pp. 365–70, at p. 368.

Just as critics continue to debate the significance of Galdós's novel, so others debate Buñuel's interpretation. For Amorós, Buñuel remains faithful to the spirit of the original work, while for Alonso Ibarrola, Buñuel's *Tristana* 'es completamente distinta a la de Galdós'.[68] While there will be those who find greater poetic justice in Buñuel's resolution of the work, however, that does not necessarily make it a more satisfying one from a feminist perspective. Indeed, in this sense, I would concur with Hans Felten's recent conclusion that 'al optar en su versión de Tristana por la solución radical, el famoso director de cine no dio un paso adelante sino un paso atrás'.[69]

While there are clearly many parallels between novel and film, it is my view that in changing the resolution of *Tristana* so dramatically, Buñuel changes the spirit of the original fundamentally. It is still a brilliant work, but it is a different one.

---

[68] José Manuel Alonso Ibarnola, 'Don Benito Pérez Galdós y el cine', *Cuadernos Hispanoamericanos*, nos 250–52 (1970–71), 650–55, at p. 654.

[69] Hans Felten, '*Tristana*: esbozo de una lectura plural', in *Benito Pérez Galdós: aportaciones con ocasión de su 150 aniversario*, ed. Eberhard Geisler & Francisco Poveadano (Frankfurt am Main: Vervuert, 1996), pp. 51–57, at p. 57

Conclusion

It is clearly impossible to come to any firm 'Conclusion' concerning the enigmatic *Tristana* and, indeed, it is hoped that this brief Guide will have raised still more questions about this intriguing text rather than attempting to offer any form of closure. For the very nature of such an ambiguous work ensures that many questions will remain unanswered, thus satisfying John Updike's demand that 'books should have secrets'.[70]

Nevertheless, as Joan Hoffman has recently stressed, the ambiguity surrounding the feminist theme in *Tristana* 'has fueled a debate that still rages among critics today' (*15*, p. 52). So perhaps the still most frequently asked question on this text should be addressed: Is *Tristana* a pro or anti-feminist novel? What follows will, of course, be based on my own interpretation of the work, which is inevitably subjective and clearly cannot be definitive. It will also be given with the qualification, as I hope the foregoing has indicated, that *Tristana* is a rich, sophisticated, and modern text for reasons apart from, albeit invariably enmeshed in, the feminist theme upon which so many critics, in the absence of any consensus, continue to deliberate.

Firstly, in attempting to answer this question, one needs a working definition of the term 'feminist'. In a recent collection of essays entitled *What is Feminism?*, Rosalind Delmar concludes: 'In the writing of feminist history it is the broad view which predominates: feminism is usually defined as an active desire to change women's position in society'.[71] This general definition echoes that of Olive Banks in *Faces of Feminism,* where she states

---

[70] Quoted by Chad Wright (*39*, p.138).

[71] Rosalind Delmar, 'What is Feminism?' in *What is Feminism?*, ed. Juliet Mitchell & Ann Oakley (Oxford: Basil Blackwell, 1986), pp. 8–33, at p. 13.

that 'those who have tried to change the position of women, or ideas about women, have been granted the title feminist'.[72]

Certainly the position of women is challenged in Galdós's *Tristana*. The question is: does the novel seek or serve to change women's position or ideas about women, or does it ultimately endorse and reinforce the *status quo*? The answer to this question, if it were answerable, would establish the novel as either pro or anti-feminist. Notwithstanding either the impossibility of a definitive answer or even its arguable irrelevance, for the purposes of this Conclusion I shall attempt an answer to this question.

As we saw in Chapter 4, narrative stance in this novel is characteristically slippery and elusive, as well as multi-layered. Indeed, as Chad Wright has recently stressed, the very fact that the narrator 'only half-tells' is, ironically, one of the aspects of the novel previously criticized which is now of particular interest to many critics *(40)*. Harold Boudreau pointed out in a study of the Galdós canon in 1990: 'Not too long ago Galdós's *Tristana* was a decidedly minor work, considered too indeterminate in a variety of ways. Then came the Buñuel movie, then came feminism, and then came the current appreciation of indeterminacy for its own sake'.[73]

The contradiction so frequently found in the narration of *Tristana* points to what Wayne Booth describes as 'an inescapable ironic invitation'.[74] Galdós's narrator plays with the reader but, as Ross Chambers explains, there is ultimately an exchange of authority as the information is given away by the narrator and received by the reader.[75]

The narrator in this novel (who shifts between omniscient and eyewitness) initially appears to sympathize almost totally with

---

[72] Olive Banks, *Faces of Feminism* (Oxford: Martin Robertson, 1981), p. 3.

[73] Harold L. Boudreau, 'The Galdós Canon', *Anales Galdosianos*, 25 (1990), 119–32, at p. 120.

[74] Wayne Booth, *The Rhetoric of Irony* (Chicago: Chicago University Press, 1974), p. 61.

[75] Ross Chambers, 'Narratorial Authority and "The Purloined Letter"' in *The Purloined Poet Lacan, Derrida and Psychoanalytic Reading*, ed. J. P. Muller & W. J. Richardson (Baltimore: John Hopkins University Press, 1988), pp. 285–306, at p. 285.

Tristana and her aspirations, which are presented as wholly reasonable and rational. She seeks equal opportunities with men to enable her to establish her own identity through professional satisfaction and economic independence, at the same time as enjoying love in a monogamous relationship: 'Libertad honrada es mi tema', she declares. As she works systematically, in her discussion with Saturna, through the various professions which might be of interest to her, Tristana is horrified and increasingly dismayed to realize not only that these professions are not open to her as a woman, but that she has received no education of any substance whatever. As I have stressed elsewhere, the problem of women's lack of education is one raised repeatedly by Galdós through his work, fictional and nonfictional, and it is reasonable to assume that this was undoubtedly one area concerning women's position which he was indeed anxious to change. If one accepts this point, then this is one aspect raised early on in the novel which points to its seeking to promote a pro-feminist argument. The fact that Tristana is shown to have ability when it comes to acquiring the knowledge and skills she so desires can be seen to reinforce this notion.

We have seen that other issues crucial to the feminist quest are focussed on in *Tristana*: those of identity and control, explored in Chapters 5 and 6. It is clear that Galdós's interest in Krausist philosophy as well as his relationships with both educated and uneducated women will have fuelled his interest in the question of female emancipation. Issues of tradition and modernity, illusion and reality, reinforced through literary and artistic allusions, are all enmeshed in Tristana's tale and in her quest for independence.

The problem arises when Tristana becomes confused. This confusion stems from a number of causes, some of which can be attributed to nature and others to nurture. This perhaps is to be expected, not only because we are reading a novel by a master of irony and ambiguity, but because the whole question of women's role in society is inherently a complex and confusing one. In the case of Tristana, of course, it is all the more complex and confusing because of her particular circumstances, graphically illustrated in her attempt to describe her relationship with don Lope: 'No estoy casada con mi marido ..., digo, con mi papá ..., digo, con ese hombre ...' (35). Silvia Tubert stresses the problem such confusion poses in the establishing of a clear identity: 'la dificultad para definir su relación con don Lope revela la ausencia de unas coordenadas claras para establecer el lugar simbólico que le corresponde a cada uno, con la consiguiente dificultad para configurar su propia identidad y asumirse como sujeto de su propio deseo' (*36*, p. 241). The confusion surrounding Tristana's proper role is intensified by the fact that, as Wright stresses, 'the values of the main narrator and the implied author appear to be strongly at odds' (*41*).

If we pause to consider the facts given by the increasingly ambivalent and unreliable narrator of her background and circumstances, there is little wonder our heroine is confused. Not only had she received an insubstantial education, but her parents were clearly both unstable. The entertaining but equally tragic account of her mother doña Josefina's decline and death might also lead the reader to speculate on the possibility of Tristana's inheriting such instability. Clearly, this experience will have had its effect upon the impressionable young girl. So closely followed by her seduction by don Lope and his deliberate manipulation and fuelling of her imagination 'con un arte sutilísimo de la palabra', it is hardly surprising that Tristana's intelligence should be clouded by confusion as well as frustration, subsequently compounded by her disillusion over Horacio and her dramatic illness.

Notwithstanding such misfortune, Tristana clings to her hopes of an independent future. Yet in her state of turmoil and desperation to regain control and gain an identity of her own, against all the odds, Tristana has been effectively mocked by some critics. Catherine Jagoe observes: 'At the crucial point when Tristana develops the tumour in her leg, there is no narrative comment whatsoever; even Horacio is silent, leaving only the feverishly bright and despairing voice of Tristana prattling on into an ominous void' (*16*, p. 134). But should Tristana be condemned or mocked for trying to remain positive in such a truly desperate situation where she is literally at death's door? Surely this is neither the aim of the (at this point) silent narrator nor the reaction of the average reader with a capacity for compassion and empathy who is witness to such 'prattling on'? The fact that she is doing so 'into an ominous void' would seem rather to intensify the sense of isolation she is suffering in this hopeless battle.

Tristana fights on until her battle is lost along with her leg, at which point she declares: 'Soy otra'. And she reverts to being 'the Other', just as tradition and don Lope would have her be: '¡Sujeta para siempre!' (87) he exclaims triumphantly. Such traditional ideals are not, of course, limited to Spain. An article just published by Alison Dakota Gee on the last survivors of Chinese foot-binding, a traditional practice which persisted through a thousand years, concludes: 'A bound-foot woman was at her most attractive when she was helpless and submissive, like a bird in a golden cage'.[76] The image is pertinent, for metaphorically Tristana's wings, as those of other Galdosian heroines before her, have been cruelly clipped.

As crutches replace her wings, Tristana's potential for independence is definitively lost, as is the hope for control over her own destiny, as she recognizes: 'No, por mucho que yo discurra, no inventaré un bonito andar con estos palitroques. Siempre seré como las mujeres lisiadas que piden limosna a la puerta de las iglesias' (104). Ruth Schmidt suggests here that 'one could say the adjective *lisiadas* is redundant, for Tristana is really identifying herself with all women' (*28*, p. 142). At this point, our heroine gives up, and Minter asks the question: 'Why should she continue to fight battles that she has won?' (*22*, p. xxiv). Yet as Tristana herself explains, '¿Qué remedio tengo más que conformarme?' (104). These are the last words we hear her speak. Minter's argument that 'to the extent that Tristana has bent don Lope to her will, she has achieved the independence so long sought' (*22*, p. xxi) implies that she is predominantly seeking the kind of power described by Cixous and discussed in Chapter 5, which is power over others rather than control over her own destiny, and this would not seem to be the case.

Now Tristana's 'prattling' voice is silent, as she herself withdraws from the 'reality' of the text which will not allow her to

---

[76] Alison Dakota Gee, 'Chinese Foot Binding: the Last Survivors Tortured for Men's Pleasure', *Marie Claire* (March 1999), pp. 25–28

establish an autonomous identity of her own.[77] Instead she is forced
to conform to the demands of patriarchal society as 'la casaron,
encasillándola dentro de un hueco honroso de la Sociedad' (110).
The *status quo* is enforced, for as Maryellen Bieder points out, 'the
non-conforming, headstrong, "masculine" female, once married, no
longer poses a threat to the stability of middle-class society'.[78] In
Livingstone's terms, of course, Tristana and don Lope are living in
harmony with the Law of Nature (*18*). But are they? Can this really
be the message of the novel and/or is this really the response of the
average reader who can hardly fail to be shocked at Tristana's
suffering and at the complete lack of poetic justice in the novel's
resolution?

It is well known that Galdós always admired women with
spirit, and for Tristana's spirit to be so cruelly crushed in this way
can hardly be seen as punishment for seeking that very self-
realization the Krausists (with whose ideas the writer had such
sympathy) had long advocated for all individuals regardless of
gender, while the patent wrong-doing of don Lope is rewarded so
richly. The narrator, no longer omniscient but privy only to certain
information, nevertheless states clearly in the opening lines of the
last chapter: 'No tuvo la vejez de don Lope toda la tristeza y soledad
que él se merecía' (109); on the contrary, we see the old man
'chupándose los dedos' in delight while Tristana, silent, looks on,
'con sumo desdén' (110).

The ending is not intended to be one of poetic justice. In my
opinion it is one that seeks at least to jolt if not to outrage the reader,
in what has been described by Farris Anderson as 'a gross parody of
marriage' and even as 'a warped comedy' (*2*, p. 74). As Joan

---

[77] James Whiston's recent study on '*Tristana y La Prensa* de Buenos Aires'
(*38*), quotes an article by Galdós published in *La Prensa* in which the
novelist criticizes 'las habladurías interminables', concluding from this that:
'En tal contexto el silencio final de Tristatna puede interpretarse como
preludio positivo a una acción comedida' (p. 196). In his view, Tristana has
found her vocation in baking cakes (p. 212).

[78] Maryellen Bieder, 'Capitulation: Marriage, not Freedom: A Study of
Emilia Pardo Bazán's *Memorias de un solterón* and Galdós's *Tristana*',
Symposium, 30 (1976), 93–109, at p. 107.

Hoffman puts it: 'Galdós wants to kill both the Angel in the House and her primary literary vehicle — the happy ending'. Hence 'the "ever-after" in this "happily-ever-after" is truly alarming' (*15*, p. 52). To accept such an ending as 'natural' is, to my mind, little more reasonable than encouraging the mutilation of Chinese women's feet by awarding the title 'Golden Lotus' to one no more than three inches in length, ensuring the near-total immobility of its owner (see note 77, above). Yet as Concepción Arenal wrote in her study of *La mujer de su casa*, wherein she saw a woman confined to the house as a mutilated being: 'Lo terrible, es que haya miles y millones que llaman perfección a la mutilación'.[79] It was the 'millones de almas oprimidas por el mismo horrible peso' whom Pardo Bazán had hoped would find freedom in *Tristana* (*24*, p. 140); instead, only a glimpse of a new, wide horizon was allowed. Yet all these images of restriction and enclosure clearly serve to reinforce the reality of life for women in nineteenth-century Spain, as Tristana soon found as 'los horizontes de la vida se cerraban y ennegrecían cada día más delante de la señorita de Reluz' (17).

It is my view that Galdós deliberately introduced the dramatic *deus ex machina* of the amputation of Tristana's leg to illustrate not only how archaic, but how wrong and unnatural, it was for women's choices and opportunities to be so curtailed. Buñuel picks up on this limitation of choice by showing Tristana deliberating over which chickpea to eat first and over which pillar was the most attractive. After her operation we see her furiously pacing up and down on her crutches like a caged animal and finally giving vent to her frustration by taking revenge on don Lope as she leaves him to die. Galdós's heroine, on the other hand, can be seen to rise above 'todo lo terrestre', upon which she looks 'con sumo desdén'. Forced into a socially acceptable role, she goes through the motions expected of her with indifference. Unlike her mother, doña Josefina, whom Partridge describes as overwhelmed with the notion that 'external reality is invading and staining her home' (*25*, p. 186), hence her obsessive rituals of cleansing and moving, Tristana has succeeded in distancing herself to the point where none of it touches her, as at the

---

[79] Concepción Arenal, *La mujer de su casa* (Madrid: Gras, 1883), p. 10.

beginning when it seemed she could 'decir a las capas inferiores del mundo físico: *la vostra miseria no me tange*' (3).

In this way, and notwithstanding 'the complicated, subversive role of the narrator(s)' (*41*), I believe Galdós has written a distinctly pro-feminist novel, in which the heroine is acknowledged as 'una mujer superior' capable, as Horacio surmises, of seeing 'un futuro que nosotros no vemos' (102). This would be in line with the author's subsequent development of 'la mujer nueva' through his contemporary drama, in which his heroine takes control not only over her own destiny but also over others.

I cannot, therefore, ultimately agree with Jagoe's conclusion that Galdós 'appropriates aspects of feminist discourse, such as the term "new woman", in the service of a conservative agenda' (*16*, p. 182). Neither can I accept the view offered by Minter of Tristana as 'a latter-day mystic' (*22*, p. xxvii). As Eric Southworth points out, 'about the state of her doctrinal convictions we have little certainty' and in his view 'Minter's account, by seemingly presenting the final conversion of the protagonist as straightforward fact, takes insufficient account of the text's ambiguity and subtle irony'(*34*). Similarly, James Whiston, while acknowledging that 'los intentos de Tristana de abrazar la modernidad son demasiados futuristas, dadas las condiciones sociales de la época' (*38*, p. 200), nevertheless concludes that 'Tristana, podría decirse, alcanza al final algo de sus aspiraciones' with her baking and that the marriage was intended as a positive example of 'modos de vivir que son más sencillos y humildes, basados en una mutualidad justa y equilibrada' (*38*, p. 213).

My own view is closer to that of Silvia Tubert who has recently stressed: 'La ironía, tan característica de la prosa galdosiana, desmiente la hipótesis de que el autor aprobaría este desenlace' (*36*, p. 237). Accordingly, my interpretation of the text is in line with Linda Willem's recent conclusion that 'the key to Galdós' feminist orientation in this text rests in its ironic narration, which covertly exposes the intolerance, injustice, and arbitrary nature of conventional social codes'.[80]

Notwithstanding all the irony and ambiguity in this tantalizing text, therefore, or perhaps because of it, it is my opinion that *Tristana* does subtly seek and potentially serve to change ideas about women and their position in society, thereby conforming to the requirements of a 'feminist' approach as defined by Rosalind Delmar in the study *What is Feminism?* quoted above. It does this by challenging the nature of the control and the limitations imposed upon women by patriarchal systems and values. The problem, as Marina Mayoral so clearly sees it, is that 'Tristana se adelanta a su tiempo por sus ideas, y no es comprendida' (*20*, p. 28). Indeed, many of Tristana's ideas concerning work, relationships, marriage, and motherhood can still be seen as modern today. Equally pertinent is her quest for an independent identity. In the work *Mujeres al alba* just published by Amnesty International on the eve of the millennium, Victoria Camps stresses the fact that: 'Desde siempre la desigualdad se ha disfrazado de una división de funciones [...] que debe desaparecer'. She closes her Prologue by quoting, in Spanish, John Stuart Mill's insistence over a century ago that 'es totalmente extraño a los valores modernos tener un estatus prescrito [...] la elección individual es ahora nuestro modelo', and commenting '"Ahora", decía Stuart Mill hace más de un siglo. Que lo citemos como una novedad en puertas del siglo XXI, y en una época caracterizada por un individualismo impenitente a otros propósitos, resulta increíble. Increíble desde la razón, pero no desde los hechos que nos golpean todos los días'.[81]

Galdós's *Tristana*, ahead of its time on a number of levels as we have seen, is at last receiving the critical attention it deserves as a novel which challenges the reader to confront both its literary and its social implications. Far from being an inferior and incomplete work,

---

[80] Linda Willem, '*Tristana* (1892)', forthcoming entry in *Feminist Encyclopedia of Spanish Literature*, ed. Janet Pérez, to be published by Greenwood Press.

[81] Victoria Camps, 'La aristocracia del sexo', Prologue to *Mujeres al alba*, ed. Victoria Camps, (Madrid: Amnistía Internacional & Alfaguara, 1999), pp. 9–13, at p. 13.

it is a carefully composed, finely tuned, and essentially modern text, which will probably continue to intrigue, inspire, and infuriate Galdós scholars well into the twenty-first century.

Bibliographical Note

1. Aldaraca, Bridget, *'El angel del hogar': Galdós and the Ideology of Domesticity in Spain* (Chapel Hill: University of North Carolina Press, 1991). Contains a considerable amount of interesting background to this phenomenon and then focusses on Galdós's treatment of it in five major novels, closing with a chapter on *Tristana* but omitting any general conclusion.

2. Anderson, Farris, 'Ellipsis and Space in *Tristana'*, *Anales Galdosianos*, 20 (1985), 61–76. Shows how ellipsis is the basic aesthetic principle that defines *Tristana* and gives it coherence and how the novel's spatial organization (specific settings and abstract space) gives form to its thematic and characterizational material.

3. Arenal, Concepción, *La emancipacion de la mujer en España* (Madrid: Ediciones Júcar, 1974). A collection of some of the first major feminist essays to be published in Spain. 'La mujer del porvenir' was written in 1861 but not published until 1868, the year of the Glorious Revolution. A tentative but nevertheless perceptive and provocative work for its time.

4. Bieder, Maryellen, 'Capitulation: Marriage, not Freedom: A Study of Emilia Pardo Bazán's *Memorias de un solterón* and Galdós' *Tristana'*, *Symposium*, 30 (1976), 93–109. Illustrates how the reader's expectations are just as let down by the conclusion of Pardo Bazán's novel as she was by that of *Tristana*, in that ultimately the dictates of society triumph.

5. Bikandi-Mejías, Aitor, *Galaxia textual: cine y literatura, 'Tristana' (Galdós y Buñuel)* (Madrid: Editorial Pliegos, 1997). Explores the myriad of intertextual points of contact between film and literature, drawing on key theoretical concepts to compare the Galdosian and Bunuelian versions of *Tristana*. Heavily theoretical; considers Buñuel's version to be as ambiguous as the original, but does not develop this provocative observation.

6. Bordons, Teresa, 'Releyendo *Tristana'*, *Nueva Revista de Filología Hispánica*, 41 (1993), 471–87. Sees *Tristana* as an early Spanish version of the 'New Woman novel' and stresses the ambiguity and irony of the narrative stance.

7. Chamberlin, Vernon, 'The Sonata Form Structure of *Tristana'*, *Anales Galdosianos*, 20 (1985), 83–96. Illustrates how the sonata form can be

seen reflected in the structure of *Tristana* by tracing analogues of the
two main competing themes of the first movement of a typical sonata,
concluding that this dictates the form of closure.

8.   Charnon-Deutsch, Lou, *Gender and Representation: Women in Spanish
     Realist Fiction* (Amsterdam: John Benjamins, 1990). A penetrating
     study of gender representation in selected novels by Valera, Pereda,
     Alas, and Galdós which argues that they are predominantly concerned
     with issues of male identity, although Galdós is credited with a greater
     understanding of sympathy towards the female conditon and psyche.

9.   Condé, Lisa Pauline, *Stages in the Development of a Feminist
     Consciousness in Pérez Galdós: A Biographical Sketch* (Lewiston, NY:
     Edwin Mellen Press, 1990). Outlines the development of Galdós's
     portrayal of women from his early novels through to his plays and final
     writings. Chapter 5 deals with the circumstances surrounding the
     creation of *Tristana*.

10. Engler, Kay, ' "The Ghostly Lover": The Portrayal of the *Animus* in
     Tristana', *Anales Galdosianos*, 11 (1977), 95–109. Sees Horacio as the
     incarnation of what Jungian psychologists call the Ghostly Lover, an
     animus figure upon whom Tristana projects her images of the ideal self,
     but ultimately fails to assimilate.

11. Friedman, Edward, '"Folly and a Woman": Galdós' Rhetoric of Irony
     in *Tristana*', *Theory and Practice of Feminist Literary Criticism*, ed. G.
     Mora and K. S. Van Hooft (Ypsilanti, MI: Bilingual Press, 1982),
     201–28. Argues that Tristana is a martyr and victim of society and that
     her defeat is a defeat for poetic justice.

12. Gold, Hazel, 'Cartas de mujeres y la mediación epistolar en *Tristana*',
     *Actas del Cuarto Congreso Internacional de Estudios Galdosianos
     (1990)* (Las Palmas: Ediciones del Cabildo Insular de Gran Canaria,
     1993), 661–71. Explores the significance of Tristana's letters on several
     levels, and particularly in relation to narrative authority.

13. Grimbert, Joan, 'Galdós's *Tristana* as a Subversion of the Tristan
     Legend', *Anales Galdosianos,* 27–28 (1992–93), 109–23. A close study
     of the links with the myth of Tristan and Iseult, showing how the
     legend is undermined by Tristana's appropriation and subsequent
     subversion of Tristan's attributes.

14. Gullón, Germán, '*Tristana*: literaturización y estructura novelesca',
     Hispanic Review, 45 (1977), 13–27. Shows how many of the literary
     allusions in the novel are designed to set up expectations in the reader
     that are subsequently thwarted, as the three protagonists take on various
     identities without ever fully realizing any of them.

15. Hoffman, Joan, 'Not So Happily Ever After: Rewriting the Courtship
     Script in *Tristana*', *Revista Hispánica Moderna*, 48 (1995), 43–54. A
     provocative study pointing out that in this novel Galdós goes so far as
     to subvert the traditional final goal of the courtship plot — the happy

marriage — inviting us to find the flaws and the injustice in this all-too-typical situation.

16. Jagoe, Catherine, *Ambiguous Angels: Gender in the Novels of Galdós* (Berkeley: University of California Press, 1994). A scholarly study on gender in Galdós's early and contemporary novels, acknowledging their ambiguity but concluding that while the writer's work became more progressive in political terms, it became increasingly conservative on 'the woman question' and appropriated 'feminist' terms for 'anti-feminist' ends.

17. Lambert, A. F., 'Galdós and Concha-Ruth Morell', *Anales Galdosianos*, 8 (1973), 33–49. Reproduces some of the letters from Concha-Ruth to Galdós, pointing to the links between the actress and Tristana and between the writer and both don Lope and Horacio.

18. Livingstone, Leon, 'The Law of Nature and Women's Liberation in *Tristana*', *Anales Galdosianos*, 7 (1972), 93–100. Argues that the novel's ending is a 'natural' and proper one and that Tristana's ambitions are totally 'unnatural'.

19. Madariaga, Benito, *Pérez Galdós: biografía santanderina* (Santander: Institución Cultural de Cantabria, 1979). Contains an interesting and informative section on the relationship between Galdós and Concha-Ruth Morell.

20. Mayoral, Marina, 'Tristana: ¿una feminista galdosiana?', *Ínsula*, 320–21 (July–August, 1973), 28. A brief but pertinent article, stressing the modernity of Tristana's ideas and the impossibility of her being able to realize them.

21. Miller, Beth, 'From Mistress to Murderess: The Metamorphosis of Buñuel's *Tristana*', in *Women in Hispanic Literature: Icons and Fallen Idols,* ed. Beth Miller (Berkeley: University of California Press, 1983), 340–59. A full and perceptive study which stresses the enigma that is Tristana and the difference in her portrayal by Buñuel, with particular reference to stock images of women.

22. Minter, Gordon (ed.), *B. Pérez Galdós: 'Tristana'* (Bristol: Bristol Classical Press, 1996). An excellent, fully annotated edition, with an interesting introduction which concludes that Tristana is a latter-day mystic with no proper outlet for her spiritual energies.

23. Miró, Emilio, '*Tristana* o la imposibilidad de ser', *Cuadernos Hispanoamericanos*, 250–52 (1970–72), 505–22. Sees the novel as a cry for individual freedom and Tristana as the helpless victim of a hostile society.

24. Pardo Bazán, Emilia, *La mujer española y otros artículos feministas*, ed. Leda Schiavo (Madrid: Editora Nacional, 1976). First published in *La España Moderna*, 17 (1890). A collection of feminist articles including studies of the work of John Stuart Mill and Concepción

Arenal and a review of *Tristana* which, in Pardo Bazán's view, promised more than it delivered.

25. Partridge, Colin, *Tristana: Buñuel's Film and Galdós' Novel: A Case Study in the Relation Between Literature and Film* (Lewiston, NY: Edwin Mellen Press, 1995). A good translation into English of Galdós's novel, followed by two brief but informative sections on the novel and the film respectively. Sees Galdós's Tristana as largely a victim of society and Buñuel's heroine as both 'Woman victimized and Woman triumphant'.

26. Pfeiffer, Erna, '*Tristana* o el poder creador de la lengua: preliminares para un análisis multidimensional de la novela', *Anales Galdosianos*, 26 (1991), 19–32. Studes the connections between the linguistic structure of *Tristana* and its thematic significance.

27. Scanlon, Geraldine, *La polémica feminista en la España contemporánea (1868–1974)* (Madrid: Siglo XXI de España Editores, 1976). An informative study on the role of women and the influence of feminism in Spain from the time of the 1868 Revolution to the end of the Franco era.

28. Schmidt, Ruth, '*Tristana* and the Importance of Opportunity', *Anales Galdosianos*, 9 (1974), 135–44. Argues that Tristana's quest for an autonomous existence is at the core of her being, and stresses how natural such a quest would be considered in the case of a man.

29. Shoemaker, William H., *The Novelistic Art of Galdós*, III (Valencia: Albatros Hispanófila, 1982). An excellent and comprehensive study of the novels of Galdós in three volumes, with a detailed section on *Tristana* in this third volume.

30. Sinnigen, John, '*Tristana*: la tentación del melodrama', *Anales Galdosianos*, 25 (1990), 53–67. Shows how the melodramatic conflict found in the original manuscript was modified through the creative process to allow for greater psychological depth, stressing the relevance of biographical factors and concluding that had the heroine been allowed to realize a truly autonomous identity, *Tristana* would not have been a realist novel but a utopian one.

31. ——, *Sexo y política: lecturas galdosianas* (Madrid: Ediciones de la Torre, 1996). Examines questions of gender, social class, and nationalism in a selection of novels from *La familia de León Roch* to *La loca de la casa*, with a brief but perceptive section on '*Tristana*: la emancipación mutilada' which concludes that Tristana continues her rebellion through her silence.

32. Smith, Gilbert, 'Galdós' *Tristana*, and Letters from Concha-Ruth Morell', *Anales Galdosianos,* 10 (1975), 91–120. Reproduces more of the letters to Galdós from Concha-Ruth and parallels a number of these with letters from Tristana to Horacio, concluding that Galdós clearly used his own personal experience as a starting point for this novel

33. Sobejano, Gonzalo, 'Galdós y el vocabulario de los amantes', *Anales Galdosianos*, 1 (1966), 85–100. Analyses the richness and variety of the lovers' language in a number of Galdós's novels, concluding that this is most abundant in *Tristana*.

34. Southworth, Eric, 'Love, Art and Religion in the Galdós of the Early 1890s: The Case of *Tristana*'. Paper to be published in the proceedings of the University of Sheffield Galdós Seminars of 1999. A challenging look at some recent interpretations of Galdós's sophisticated use of art in this novel, and the implications in relation to love and beliefs.

35. Tsuchiya, Akiko, 'The Struggle for Autonomy in Galdós' *Tristana*', *Modern Language Notes*, 104 (1989), 330–50. A breakthrough article which illustrates Galdós's sophisticated use of an ironic narrator and concludes that the withdrawal of Tristana's voice from the text corresponds to her triumph over reality.

36. Tubert, Silvia, '*Tristana:* ley patriarcal y deseo femenino', *Bulletin of Hispanic Studies* (Glasgow), 76 (1999), 231–48. A stimulating study which focuses on female desire and its conflict with traditional female roles in society, alongside the inherent fragility of patriarchal notions of 'masculinity'.

37. Valis, Noël, 'Art, Memory and the Human in Galdós' *Tristana*', *Kentucky Romance Quarterly*, 31 (1984), 207–20. Sees the role of art in *Tristana* as a crucial one, moulding and transforming personality, aided by an increasing loss of control over memory.

38. Whiston, James, '*Tristana* y *La Prensa* de Buenos Aires', in his *Creatividad textual e intertextual en Galdós,* Ottawa Hispanic Studies, 22 (Ottawa: Dovehouse Editions, 1999), pp. 188–213. Examines links between articles written by Galdós for *La Prensa* and his fictional text, *Tristana*, highlighting in particular attitudes towards work. Whiston sees this as a central theme in the novel and relevant to the ending, where he considers both Tristana and don Lope to be busily and happily occupied. This is one chapter in a study of selected texts of Galdós, incorporating a considerable amount of original research and manuscript study.

39. Wright, Chad, 'The vision of Corporal Fragmentation in Galdós's *Tristana*', *A Sesquicentennial Tribute to Galdós, 1843–1993*, ed. Linda M. Willem (Newark, DE: Juan de la Cuesta, 1993), pp. 138–54. Explores the multiple images of dismemberment, malfunctioning, and disarticulation in the novel, stressing that the body has its own discourse and that Tristana's discourse is amputated with her leg. Concludes that *Tristana* is Galdós's most searching study of woman's place in the world and also more closely related to the penetrating analysis of the Generation of 1898 than his earlier works.

40. ——, 'Going in Circles: Repetition and the Reader in Galdós's *Tristana*'. Unpublished paper given at the Midwest Modern Languages

Association Conference, Chicago, in 1991. Explores the system of images, shapes, patterns, and sounds that denote the circle which, as a sign, is multivalent and ambiguous in this novel.

41. ——, ' "Tan misteriosa autoridad": Narrative Authority in Galdós's *Tristana', Anales Galdosianos* (in press). Examines the novel as an exercise in narrative technique and concludes that, among Galdós's works, none is a greater puzzle than *Tristana*.

CRITICAL GUIDES TO SPANISH TEXTS

Edited by
Alan Deyermond and Stephen Hart

CRITICAL GUIDES TO SPANISH TEXTS

Edited by
Alan Deyermond and Stephen Hart